Football's Poetic Licence

Joe Morris

Copyright © 2022 by Joseph David Morris

All rights reserved. No part of this book may be reproduced or used in any manner without written permission of the copyright owner except for the use of quotations in a book review. For more information, address: nathanielcourt20@outlook.com

FIRST EDITION

ISBNs:
Paperback: 978-1-80227-869-9
ebook: 978-1-80227-870-5

CONTENTS

Sunday, Sunday 1
East London Horror Show 4
Kick Off Again 9
It was 56 Years Ago Today 15
Terry Neill Dies: An Irish Legend 20
Another Italian West Ham Striker 23
Football on the Horizon. 26
Yet More Football. 28
You'll Never Guess. 31
Jesse Lingard 35
Now Here's the Story So Far 37
Remember Those Days 42
Macca and Liverpool 46
Albania's Finest at West Ham? 49
Summer. 52
Hungary and England 56
Ken Aston: My primary school headmaster 58
Thomas Hardy and Football 63
Forest back in the big time. 65
The last post. 67
Paris — Champions League Final 68
The close season. 71
The finishing line. 75
Mark Noble 78

Merseyside Glory	79
The Premier League Season's End	85
The Last Euro Adventure	90
Real Madrid again in Champions League Final	91
Premier League End of Season Ups and Downs	96
Hammers Need Another Euro comeback	103
Premier League Final Stages	107
Gazza	111
Derby, the Neutrals Feel for You	114
Sean Dyche Sacked at Burnley	115
Hammers in Euro Semi-final	119
Hammers 1-1 after Euro League Battle Royale	122
Hammers Chew Up Stickier Toffees	125
World Cup draw	130
International Friendlies	132
Russian Euros? Surely Not	135
West Ham Beaten in Local Derby	137
West Ham — What a Team	140
City Still Top	143
My Dad	148
West Ham in Europe	152
Premier League review	156
FA Cup Fifth Round	160
Chelsea's Russian revolution	162
Football grounds	165

Manchester City Beaten	168
Don't Stop West Ham	169
Liverpool Beat Inter Milan	173
City as Slick as Ever	176
Ilford FC	182
The Voice of the FA Cup	186
What, No Football Tomorrow?	189
The Rams Take a Battering	192
City — Still Flying	194
1966 and All That	197
Rafa — Sacked and Not Backed	201
Boris: More Rugby Than Football	205
The Old Days at Upton Park	208
The FA Cup Giant Killers and The Hammers	212
FA Cup Again — Hammers vs. Leeds Third Round	217
Hornets Stung by the Hammers	222
Woe, West Ham, Never on Boxing Day	225
Out of the Carabao Cup, But Who Cares?	228
The First World War Football Truce	231
Virus Claims Football Before Christmas	234
Football at Christmas Always Seemed Too Much	237
Chelsea – Leeds: Another Fiery Contest	240
Goalless Draw at Burnley for the Hammers	242
My Grandpa Jack: West Ham Supporter	244
World Cup — a Year Away Now	246
FA Cup Second Round Again	250

Ray Kennedy 252
What Would Peter Jones AND Bryon Butler
Have Thought? 254
For West Ham Read the Class of '65 256
In The Middle of Europe 258
New Managerial Brooms — Gerrard, Howe and
Smith 259
The San Marino Rout 262
West Ham in the Top Three 264
To FA Cup Glory 266
FA Cup Final Day 269
Euros 2020 271
Honours Even in London Derby 273

SUNDAY, SUNDAY

Oh, Sunday, Sunday
Used to be the day of the week
When players used to be meek
Ever so sleek
But tough as teak
Then West Ham discovered
Although never recovered
From their fourth consecutive Sunday
It had to be this day
This time at Villa Park
Ready to be on the mark
I've never been one to complain
About late summer sun poised to wane
First there was City at home
Leave your grievances alone
Then Forest found a sun-dappled spot
Hammers beaten, surely not
And then to make matters worse
When most of us thought there had been a curse
Brighton visited the East End
How we were driven round the bend

Oh, Sunday, Sunday
Please refrain from this day
Sundays were days of rest
After the week provided the ultimate test
When the tools of labour

Prompted our neighbour
To take sympathy and pity
West Ham now away from the City
2 o clock in yet more fields
Brandishing yet more shields
Of claret and blue
When David Moyes and you
Will wonder why they can
Please, please no longer, there has to be a ban
Eat your roast
Make a toast
For Sundays when
Sir Geoff once mowed his grass in his den
After '66 World Cup glory
That perfect story
But Villa it is on the Sabbath day of recreation
Across the nation
Noisy neighbours Spurs
Next weekend
On Saturday perhaps please send
Some welcome respite
No more spite
Just a three o'clock kick off tomorrow
No more sorrow
Just tradition and conflict
Don't inflict
Sunday lunchtime
Yorkshire pudding and wine
Football be kind

Make sure the Irons don't fall behind
Propping up the top flight
Every single night
On the hour
Singularly lacking in fire power
Through to the group stage
On the next page
Of Euro Conference
Now here's a reference
To misquote the Stranglers
No more wranglers
On Sunday anymore
Just Saturday for a while
With considerable style.

EAST LONDON HORROR SHOW

|Oh, to be of a claret and blue disposition
A hat-trick of disasters
A cacophony of calamities
Reckless defending
West Ham, bottom of the Premier League
No points, no goals
Spineless, still dazed
Crocodile tears and no sympathy
Slumbering in late August
Soporific warmth and heat
Dozing in the lengthening shadows
Where summer has now left her blissful legacy on the year
West Ham, now reminiscent
Of an ancient listed building
Forgotten by progress and beaten up
Discarded like an old Benson & Hedges cigarette
On the old Upton Park Chicken Run
Weather beaten and haggard
What happened to the world-beating Hammers of last season?
Surely just a blip
We must hope so
Now just grotesquely distorted
As those ugly images at fairground mirrors
Time for stern re-appraisals for David Moyes
Serious training ground discussions
Seven new signings but three no-shows

Don't panic but be wary
Of relegation rumours and vultures
Bats in the belfry
Lost in the Forest
Overwhelmed by City gents of the Premier League
Champions variety
And now defeated by end of pier seaside entertainers
Gulls swooping voraciously
On London Stadium chips
Brighton, breezy, carefree
West Ham, jinxed and hoaxed
By Potter's finest ceramic figures of well-crafted professionalism
Maybe enough said
Meanwhile Arsenal head the Premier League
In its infant cries
Three out of three
Opening salvoes
Gunners' grapeshot
Firing on cliched cylinders
Nine goals against the residents
Of the palatial Palace
Then outfoxing the Leicester Light Brigade
Brendan Rodgers can only fantasise
About another Premier League trophy
Then another seaside stroll for the galloping Gunners
Beside the red and black deckchairs of Bournemouth
Spurs on the shoulders of their North London rivals
Blowing fiercely down their noisy neighbours' necks

Wolves hounded by the past
Palace off the mark properly
Against the clueless Villa
Steven Gerrard struggling for crumbs of comfort
But finding none
Whitewashed Villa now tarnished by the weekend
Claret and blue stains
And the Villa Park slump
Temporary, they must hope
Lampard's Everton
Still in turmoil, crisis
Partially lifted by a point
Against the hunters and gatherers in the Forest
Where Cloughie once worked the oracle
Tangled weeds and bushes
Now cleared for a profitable return to Premier League shores
Fulham also back in the big time
The Cottagers' industry is alive and well
Edging London derby
With fellow neighbours
Brentford in five goal humdinger
Deep in the Cottage but far from overawed
This time Fulham will drop their anchor
Securely tied to their Craven Cottage moorings
In Premier League safety
They must wish with bated breath
Foxes of Leicester
Beaten by those saintly Saints of Southampton
Brendan Rodgers

Must be hoping for religious salvation
Premier League winners
Now just a prehistoric footnote
Manchester City surprisingly held to six goal thriller
By high tempo Newcastle
Eddie Howe's Geordie black and white striped army
Seemingly on the verge of a bright and lustrous era
Revitalised and refurbished
By millions of Saudi money
Defeats now inexcusable
And finally Leeds
With the Midas touch
Of an American in Yorkshire
Elland Road slowly stretching the aching limbs
Off a tortured past of the Championship and League One
Jesse, this is your time
To seize that celebrated day
Over the weekend
Leeds beat Chelsea
Now that used to be a fixture to treasure
And will be once again
Chopper Harris eyeballing Norman 'Bites Yer Legs' Hunter
With lingering menace
Through the seasons
Leeds now score their own personal hat-trick
Against the Chelsea without the billions
Of Russian oligarchical money
That once washed over Stamford Bridge
Like a crashing tidal wave

Premier League back-to-back winners
But the waters are cascading down the terraces and posh seats
An interesting turn of events
Chelsea may have lost their focus
Yet your Hammers are sinking rapidly
Marooned and stranded at the bottom
Seeking light at the end of the tunnel.

KICK OFF AGAIN

After 120 plus years of hostility, adversity
And truly remarkable achievements
Picture postcards of triumphant league titles
And horrific promotion and relegation
Pain and pleasure
The fascinating extremes
But it's Sunday evening
And the Premier League has yielded its certainties, predictabilities
And, yes, you've guessed it
Inevitabilities
Oh, what sweet joy
Palace are broken into
By the brutal ammunition
Of Gunners firing flamboyant flares
Accurate missiles
Arsenal, opening up the first page
Of their picturesque prose and verse
A profusion of perfect diction
Page after page
Of theatrical movement
Melodic reminders
Of Wenger's Invincibles
Patient and sharply
Innovative, passing
Refreshingly ambitious
Could be contenders

Meanwhile Bournemouth
Inspired by invigorating bracing seaside air
Beat Villa at the Vitality
Steven Gerrard with homework and revision
To concentrate the mind
Then Fulham
Once mocked by the cynics
For their lack of buoyancy
Back in the top flight
After sliding from view
Into the darker waters of the Championship
Just for a season
Everton
Relieved to be amongst the earls and dukes
Of the Premier League elite
Fulham though
Silencing the Anfield rap
Jurgen's Liverpool
Held to ransom
But still jaundiced
And poorly under the weather
Too much heat
And sun
And heightened hopes
Everton, though
Where once Goodison was once the Bank of England
Now possibly a high street building society
Some would say
A farcical charade

A freak show
Of harlequins and court jesters
Jugglers and acrobats
In the big top
But Frank Lampard
Will attempt to be
A capable pair of hands at the tiller
Beaten by a Chelsea
Without Russian trappings of luxury and affluence
Moody, brooding
Sulky Lukaku
But still a goal
Too much for Everton to handle
And now Leeds
Maybe a contradiction in terms at times
Neither hot nor cold
Brilliant and breath-taking
From a historical perspective
Before plunging to the bottom of the well in League One
An embodiment of disasters
But yesterday brand new
Respectable, spick and span
It's amazing what an American can do
In the heart of Yorkshire
Jesse Marsch as opposed to James
Flinging open the Wild West saloon doors
'Get me a bourbon, barman'
Leeds devour the latest pack of hungry Wolves
Old gold but never ominous

Leeds leading the way
And models of resurgence
Back where they belong
Newcastle finally breathing fire
And full of intoxicating ales from Geordie breweries
Overcome Forest, back amongst the big boys
Where once Cloughie delivered sermons and lectures
Loved by the purists
Who believed too
That football should be played on the grass
Rather than next to the old Concorde
Or jumbo jets at the highest altitude
And then Spurs
Now there's an interesting case
Microscopically analysed
Attacked viciously in one breath
Before handsomely despatching
Less than saintly Saints
With a dismissive sweep
Of both feet and head
Utterly contemptuous
Bombast and bumptious
Revelling in August splendour
First day of the season grandeur
Farewell, Southampton
Four goals of supreme quality
Tottenham out of the blocks
Like the nearby Harringay Greyhounds in the old days
Leicester fair to middling

Honours even
At the King Power
With charming Brentford
Still living on old wartime anecdotes
But now modern forward thinking, go ahead
Playing football under the sweetest Danish
Icing on the cake
Inspired by the right directors and producers
Lovely choreography
Perfectly conceived and executed
By men of honour
Finally Manchester United
Oh, woe again
Surely this is a Greek tragedy
Beaten at Old Trafford
Bountiful, breezy Brighton
No saucy postcards
Or seaside humour
Just a Potter moulding the finest material
Not quite a crisis for United
But Accident and Emergency are ready and waiting
Manchester United lose to Brighton
On day one
Liverpool not quite up to their Saturday lunchtime best
Room for improvement
One and all
Finally, City, perhaps
Just stately and leisurely
At the London Stadium

Champions always know how to pace themselves
Winning without moving out of first gear
West Ham still reflecting
On last season's European jaunts
Not quite at the proverbial races
Basking in Mediterranean sweltering Fahrenheits
Beaten but far from bowed
37 games to go.

IT WAS 56 YEARS AGO TODAY

It was 56 years ago today
And nothing since
England won their only World Cup to the day
When memories were children
But now lost in the mists of time
Like an ancient crisp bag or bottle of pop
Like a mournful dirge
A sad and tear-stained funeral
All of those rose coloured days
That day of significance
Weighty gravitas
July 30, 1966
Victorious
But left behind sorrowfully
In the slipstream of history
Just a footnote, passing mention
Of a fond recollection
Simply that
Riotous celebration
In isolation
Burst balloons and flattened party hats
56 years of hurt
Rejection, foolhardiness
Questions
A mountain of questions
No more theatre
Neither drama nor ecstasy

Falling flat like a 70-year-old bottle of champers
A destitute nation
Grieving
But not the end of the world
Burying gnarled hands in grave despair
Nowhere to go
Nor comfort to cling to
A snapshot of the 1960s
Reduced to a microcosm
A faint, flickering heartbeat
That throbbed powerfully on one day
When Britain
Longing for their day of fame and celebrity
Were rewarded for their patience
Since the first infant cries of the Jules Rimet World Cup
When Uruguay passed the baton down the generational line
For Brazil, Germany, Argentina, Spain and Italy to claim
As their divine right
But it's been 56 years
Since momentous echoes drifted regretfully
Down the hallways, pavilions and corridors of our hopes and dreams
Nothing but hapless managers and coaches
With lonely trudges towards the exit door
What an empty, hollow vacuum
Drained of colour, fallow failure
Almost but not quite at times
But too tantalisingly close
And yet Bobby lifted the World Cup at Wembley

Chaired on the shoulders
Of Sir Geoff, Nobby, Alan Ball,
Sir Martin Peters, Roger Hunt, Jack and Bobby Charlton
And then there were the haunting ghosts
Of 56 years ago
Just over half a century
The shame and guilt overwhelming us
Like a storm-tossed ocean
And yet why the post mortems
And probing inquests
The excuses, lands of alibi, detailed critique
Analysing the obvious
The fact remains though
That Sir Geoff did score a hat-trick
And the Germans were lulled into a false sense of security
Levelling the game with only seconds left
And then extra time beckoned
Sir Alf, defiant to the end
Screeched out the beseeching cry
'You've won it once
So do it again'
When energy and desire seemed to be crumbling like the
Roman Empire
Where was Gibbon when we needed him most?
Then with the receding tides
Of a North London afternoon had faded
Off into some desolate wasteland
Bobby slowed the game
To his measured specifications

While Jack Charlton and Alan Ball
With the blond one from Barking
So noble and regal
Pleaded with the claret and blue skipper
To dump the ball into a far distant county, shire, town and village
Where none could retrieve the game
The Germans, frozen in movement
Blunted and dulled
Like a thousand school pencils, nonplussed
Beaten on the day
England lift the Jules Rimet Cup
World champions at last
But destiny would have other plans
No more warriors or mud spattered heroes anymore
Just the one World Cup
Soul destroying
But we'll always have Qatar at the end of the year
More World Cup scripts, manuscripts
Drafts, first chapters
Documentary proof
That Gareth Southgate could emulate the template
Of disbelieving Sir Alf who
Upon the final whistle 56 years ago
Sat impassively as if he'd lost a dearly beloved
Solemn, a phlegmatic figure
Framed in shock perhaps
For 1966 read 2022
It happened today

Historians have little time though for warm sentiment
Go out in the desert, Gareth
And do it again
In our lifetime
Thank you for being here in the moment.

TERRY NEILL DIES: AN IRISH LEGEND

And so, we remember the passing
Of an Irish legend
On the cusp of becoming an octogenarian
Pride of place within the marbled halls of Arsenal's Highbury
Terry Neill, a yeoman of the guard
A sterling defender
A bastion of red-blooded robustness
Strong, impassable
A green brick wall of impregnability
Northern Ireland will mourn this tower of strength
Through the tempestuous bloody battles of the IRA
When none could silence the heartache and suffering
Of the eternally witty and lyrical people of Belfast and the Shankhill Road
Lovely people who just wanted to live under the warm blanket
Of peace and love
Neill arrived at Arsenal
And fastened himself securely to the folklore once spread
By the Boy Bastin, Hapgood
The elusive and delightful Alex James
Then Neill encountered Brady
Liam Brady
And sighed with religious reverence
Brady, so young but replete

With originality and heaven-sent talent
Then out of the corner of Neill's eye
Peter Storey, Jon Samuels, Eddie Kelly, George Graham
Too good to be true
A festival and carnival had arrived in Neill's vision
Then there were the managerial years at Arsenal
Three consecutive FA Cup Finals
Defeat in '78 by the country folk
Of Suffolk's Ipswich Town
Roger Osborne stunned and overcome in rhapsodies
of blue
He did score the winning goal
But Arsenal quickly erased these horrendous Wembley
images from their mind
A year later
Arsenal return to the scene of the crime
And narrowly edge an epic five goal thriller against the
world
Famous and fabled Manchester United
A delicious concoction of Irish stews
Frank Stapleton, David O'Leary and Liam Brady
Intoxicate the soul and the palate
Then in 1980, a knight of the realm
Now stooped to conquer
With claret and blue signatures
Sir Trevor Brooking
Unlikely and physically improbable
West Ham, through and through
A headed winner so low down

On the grass and soil of Wembley's green acres
That couldn't have happened
Terry Neill, gracious in defeat
But still smiling at the romantic pages of Wembley past
Finally, Neill commits the cardinal sin
Crossing the great North London divide
Surely a rush of blood to the head
Boss at Spurs, the ultimate footballing betrayal
Breaking Arsenal hearts
How dare he
Unforgivable surely
But let bygones be bygones
Terry Neill full of Irish mellowness and the blarney
A man of engaging honesty
A quick quip or joke for the Clock End at Highbury
Still unmistakably Arsenal
Through and through.

ANOTHER ITALIAN WEST HAM STRIKER

At long last
Another claret and blue striker
West Ham strike gold
With another Italian stallion
Ladies and gentlemen
Gianluca Scamacca
Now they say that
After a wholesome plate of pasta and spaghetti
The land which once gave the world the prolific Paolo Rossi
By World Cup assignment
A natural goal scorer with a ravenous appetite
And a modern satnav
For the location of goals, goals, goals
But now in the simmering and sweltering heat of a
British July summer
West Ham land their very own Italian job
Scamacca from Sassuolo
You'll have to forgive the geographical ignorance
But enlightenment required
Sassuolo?
Somewhere on the heel of Italy but not its ankle
Unknown and unheralded
But 23, ready and prepared
Hungry for London Stadium approval
Accepted by those with a homage to pie and mash
A reception to remember

Italian international
But wet behind the ears
If he has any of Paolo Di Canio's endowments
But without the temperamental eruptions
It could be an East End season to admire
On any claret and blue mantelpiece
A fortnight before we kick off once again
And bodies are trickling into the Hammers' academy
Joining the club which
Next week
Now 56 years ago so we are now painfully reminded
Provided the vertebrae of England's only World Cup representation
As outright winners
When Mooro, Sir Geoff and Sir Martin once gilded the lily
Crowned world champions
With Trafalgar Square fountains of praise and rapture
Flooding the nation's streets and beaches
Seaside esplanades
How good to be patriotically English
Oh, what a night that must have been
But now West Ham give us our first Italian for a while
A saint and angel
We hope
Goals from every hypotenuse
Every compass point
Pythagoras' theorem
Inside frenetic penalty areas
From the halfway line

As long as the new Italian East Ender
Makes his emphatic presence felt
Volleyed goals with violent vehemence
Bulging oppositions' nets with addictive frequency
Gianluca, the stage is yours
We can hardly wait
Accompanied perhaps by Filip Kostic from Frankfurt
Overlapping wing back
Or excitingly, brilliantly, what a scoop
Lozano, a Mexican
From the land of melodious mariachi
It all sounds like preposterous wishful thinking
But, West Ham, allow us this moment
Of picturesque Premier League landscapes
Where fortunes fly
And even Manchester City cry
While the Hammers' dreamers
Continue to aspire
Fellow football bards
Certainly no yellow or red cards
It's a privilege to be in your company
To all of my fellow football poets
You're all brilliant and exceptional.

FOOTBALL ON THE HORIZON

Football, on the horizon once more
Like the passing of the seasons
Football, like the clock on the wall
Ticking towards the passions of the teeming terraces
The fans return to their natural place in the scheme of things
Wending their way
Traipsing towards those timeless turnstiles
Heaving with hope
Sunlit tunnels
At the other end of August to May
Refrains of old, collective chants and new
Chanting the melodies that Uncle and Dad once intoned
Through cloth capped caps
Then Mum once offered her knitted hats
Days when rattles and rosettes flashed
With transient pleasure
Then contorted faces of weather-beaten defeat
Oh, the loss
But then the sudden transition to victory on Cup Final day
The culmination of it all
But on this Saturday, Sunday and Monday
The random nature of times, dates
Any chronological order
Who cares
Play the Beautiful Game at midnight
Don't wake up the neighbours
Because the supporters will embrace the hour yet again

In the first grievances of the world
Swirl when people bristle at the injustices
Groaning at ongoing discomfort on the theatrical stages of life
But hey, we'll always have football at any time of your choosing
The green carpet of August
Hostilities
Then the millionaires of football's monied classes
Preside from on high
While those below flourish their scarves
Cheering under the canopy
Huddled together, cold
Warm, the Bovril masses gathered
The sound of those who may never be quiet
For a single moment
Bound together by vested interests
The fusion of blood ties, wit and humour
Wandering through our fevered thoughts
For we were biased
Devoted to forlorn causes
Relegation and promotion
Goals that lighten our moods
Because we were there
Bitten fingernails to the bitter end
Timeless and priceless
This is our time to win the League
Now or never time frames
Hopefully savouring the wine
Of triumphant times.

YET MORE FOOTBALL

Football now almost at the height of summer
When cricket blades and tennis rackets
Shimmered through the haze in a stunned daze
Last night Italy and England meet up in a revolving door
Haven't they met before?
This was familiarity
Breeding indifference
Who cares about this inconsequential non event
Too many questions
About necessity and importance
UEFA Nations League
It sounds like a convenient excuse
For kick abouts on the beach
Between the nations of the world
On sand-kissed Mediterranean shores
Flip flops and Crocs padding leisurely
Along whispering waters where the sea meets the ocean
And the players of the Premier League
Massage battered cruciates
And the aching limbs of winter
Where once tackles flew
Like gulls swooping down from afar
But Italy and England were still playing that old song
That August to May sonata
Where passes were like more illustrations in our mind
Precise as maths equations

Could somebody please give a synopsis or detailed explanation
Of the UEFA Nations League?
The brainchild of somebody with too much time on their hands
Hard and cruel, but quite possibly true
And an international at Molineux
Now that had to be a first
Or the first since 1950s rock and roll
A fleeting meeting with famished Wolves
Foraging for scraps
Still scratching our June heads
Bemused, confused
A goalless draw, just a mystery
Some indecipherable code
Enigmatic as football in June
Sheer madness
Gareth Southgate
Faintly apologetic
For lack of English firepower
But Gareth, it is summer
And England are in the Elysian Fields of Trent Bridge
And cricket rules the roost
Make plans for
Exotic bars, sangria
Heavenly haciendas
Chirruping Spanish cicadas
Warm nights amongst the hypnotic fans and flamencos
Rest tired bodies

Tammy Abraham, Phil Foden
Raheem Sterling, Declan Rice
Trent Alexander Arnold, Kieran Trippier
And the immensely gifted Jack Grealish
The football season had completed its exams
During the middle of last month
There are no more prizes, incentives, medals
Put your feet up for just a while
Nurse your groin strains
Beleaguered ankles, joints, gigantic bank balances
Adjust the designer sunglasses
Preservation orders on pina coladas
Protect the luxuries of life
Watch the apricot sun sink
Over varnished bodies
Like mahogany cabinets ready for another coat
Stop the football carousel
UEFA Nations League
Surely meaningless and possibly too profound for words
August is our Premier League story
Chapters galore.

YOU'LL NEVER GUESS

You'll never guess
It isn't conjecture
Guess work
Surmising on what could happen
The land of hyperbole could be the truth
It's happened
Ladies and gentlemen
Stunning announcement
Another new face at the London Stadium
Time to go crazy
Celebrate indefinitely
Dance around lamp posts
Rejoice in street parties
Claret and blue klaxons
West Ham reveal new signing
Hold the back page
Brace yourself in Barking
And burst open the bubbly in Dagenham
This is an epoch-making moment
As momentous as that pivotal day
At the end of this month in 1966
When Sir Robert Moore
Wiped his hands on purple
And then lifted the World Cup
The Jules Rimet trophy
In the safe keeping of West Ham hands
For Bobby was homegrown

And now we discover
Flynn Downes grew up
With claret and blue in his blood, soul
Breathing in the Upton Park ozone layer
Heart beating with all those lovely palpitations
When Sir Geoff scored
Pop Robson wheeled away in delight
In familiar goal scoring attire
Flynn Downes
He glided nonchalantly away from the other Swans
But then came home
To be amongst his claret and blue brethren
Suddenly the floodgates could be about to open
In Stratford's grandest abode
We couldn't possibly tell you
Where? How? Who?
Flynn Downes is the West Ham new kid on the block
Unknown and obscure
But now thrust into the full glare
Of Premier League prominence, poised
And yet it can't be denied
He sounds like a throwback
To the days when young blood would pass
Through the Upton Park portals
To little fanfare
And questions about identity and whereabouts
Unheard of, unheralded
Brentwood born
Where once Sir Trevor Brooking settled his mortgage

And lay down his perfect tools of craftsmanship
And England was privileged for so many years
So, Downes, a boyhood Hammer
Essex in his genetic makeup
Destined for glorious deeds
Hopefully, maybe encouragingly
The finest of them all
In years to come
On YouTube, you discover
Uncanny resemblances to Declan and Bobby
Upright, imposing as the London Stadium itself
So, it's Flynn Downes for a couple of million
A few bob as they say
In the modern vernacular
Now for the indecisive Jesse Lingard
Dithering and delaying
Perhaps more concerned with Hollywood multi-million dollars
On fields of America
David Moyes
May we heartily suggest
Youri Tielemans or Sarr from Watford
Far more inclined to don the Irons' claret and blue
Jesse Lingard
Some would call him
That typical football mercenary
With designs on the American brand and franchise
Hanging out with the Yankees
Strike one with baseball

In his ears and eyes
But to all Hammers
Feverishly anticipating Flynn Downes
Here lies the potential
Of the best signing of the summer
Still 23 and a spring chicken
Coltish and receptive
To the guiding principles of the West Ham academy
David Moyes
Your supporters await
Another set of diamonds and rubies
Fresh, eager, buoyant
Committed to the cause
This has all the makings
Of a season to remember
You never know.

JESSE LINGARD

To be Jesse Lingard
Or not to be Jesse Lingard
That is the question
Whether it be nobler to suffer
The slings and arrows
Of outrageous wage demands
A mind motivated by dirty lucre
The filthy obscenity of excessive wealth
Distorted by money
Polluted by the stench of hundreds and thousands
Millions no less
Of floating reams of fivers, tenners
Twenties, fifties
A mountainous multitude of more and more
Unimaginable, barely believable riches
And yet we knew
Jesse Lingard is clearly concerned only with financial security
Rather than footballing prowess
Feathering nests now rather than later
Pampered impossibly
From those early days at United
Of course, the superstar
When Sir Alex
Bestowed upon Lingard
The accolades and adulation of youth
But now Lingard stifled and overwhelmed

By his overweening ego
Now Forest join in
With the great auction market
Brian Clough, of course
Brought us the first million pound
Trevor Francis
But now Lingard falls headlong into the net of temptation
The astonishing spectre of 200 grand a week
A moral maze of abomination
The repulsive greed
Football strangled
By rampant desire
Thousands of noughts in bank balances
Throttled
By the grasping hands of capitalism
But before you sign
On the dotted line
Jesse Lingard
Just remember the London Stadium fans
Who just want you to play
Rather than build up your accumulating fortunes
And then Lingard found his clearing in the Forest
Hammered into history
Claret and blue
No longer in the Irons' vision anymore.

NOW HERE'S THE STORY SO FAR

Now here's the story so far
Football's baffling and head spinning ambiguities
The lack of clarity
The familiar adjectives
When transfer gossip reaches its loudest crescendo
The strange pronouns
The repetitive descriptions
For instance, wait for it
West Ham are closing in
On player A or B
Even C
Closing in on signings
Suggestions of stealthy movements in the undergrowth
Approaching their prey
Sneaking covertly
With suspicion perhaps
Or possibly hunting down said player in captivity
Endangered species
Under threat of extinction
Ready to be caught and arrested, perhaps
Loitering with intent in the neighbourhood
The hush hush
Clandestine operations
Of the July transfer window
Broja interested in move to West Ham
Then Chelsea

Change their mind once again
Broja has preferences
Irons in the fire
That's appropriate
Broja from adorable Albania
Remain where you are
You're going precisely nowhere
Then there are the advanced negotiations
That are so close to resolution
You can almost touch and feel them
Are they so advanced you can barely see them
Over football's idyllic scenery?
Perhaps they're over the rural hills
Far and away
Somewhere in deepest middle England
Where football fans gather their thoughts
And plan their expeditions
For next season's home and away
August opening day of the season
Inevitabilities
Then there are the talks this summer
Over dozens of players
How enormously flattered they must be
To be spoken of in glowing terms
Discussions of fees
All the minutiae of agents wrangling over their cut
For their prized assets
Millions of pounds whirring in their eyes
Like those seaside amusement arcades

On those delightful one-armed bandits
Yesterday the 20-year-old Albanian
Nurtured by Chelsea
Is considered as a reasonably likely claret and blue
acquisition for the Hammers
But then the probable becomes the highly unlikely
It's all open to interpretation
Since Broja is highly desirable
But no longer reasonably likely
So, that's final
Or a moderate possibility yet to be clarified
Before the tug of war
Between the parent club falls on stony ground
Finally, round the clock talks become a subdued whisper
All change of heart and mind
Summon Broja back into Chelsea's greatest and latest
And yet again Jesse Lingard is still 'wanted' by David
Moyes
Implying the Wild West baddie
Stealing from banks in cowboy mode
Then we discover that West Ham
Would love James Ward Prowsc
To be in their well-equipped ranks
Big name midfielders as opposed to little names
From some remote spot of Britain
And finally supporters will be buzzing
Like those traditional bees of summer
Or the dancing wasps that dart in and out
Of balmy hawthorn bushes

Or glorious yellow and red roses
Of the football summer pre-season hullabaloo
Last night the sleepy suburb of Hertfordshire
Awoke to Boreham Wood
Holding claret and blue
To the most honourable of 1-1 draws
A minor shock
But friendlies should never be a barometer of any form
Since this is the dress rehearsal
For more dramatic contests of Premier League substance
And finally the Suffolk Tractor Boys of Ipswich are
banished to the side lines
Defeated
But hopeful of a renaissance one day
In exalted company at the top table of the Premier
League's feasting grounds
When Sir Bobby Robson
Once trod the sacrosanct green grass of Portman Road
But we prepared for football
And its linguistic complexity
When signings are talks
Or just advanced in their thinking
Closing in, waiting to pounce
Almost but not quite over the line
Or the goal line in which case
VAR in friendlies
Now that's an excellent idea
But back in the transfer window
Multi-billion pound superstars

With extortionate billions on their mind
At the right time and place
Football's lovely literature
Never ceases to wonder
Keep waiting for golden boys, West Ham.

REMEMBER THOSE DAYS

You must remember those days of yore
When we were the burgeoning age of four
On the streets and roads
Where we unlocked the codes
Of youth and childhood
Or maybe we could
In rags and clothes with holes
Certainly not bowls
Over and over again
The pavement and the fen
Rush goalie, three and in
Next to the welcoming bin
With tin cans and rolled up paper
The interminable caper
We rushed about furiously
Albeit curiously
Scampered and scurried
Permanently hurried
Man on, I'm unmarked
Oh, how we larked
Give me the ball, Joe
Please don't go slow
Only the goalkeeper to beat
Score, Joe, stay on your feet
Cross the ball, my friend
On my head, the free kick bend
Mum's calling us in for tea

But don't forget me
Hit it on the volley and half volley
Avoid that neglected trolley
The supermarket kind
Never a bind
But we loved the game
Not a hint of shame
Joe, beat the offside trap
No crowd applause or clap
Just the innocence of youth
We were never uncouth
Coats for goalposts
We were the perfect hosts
Our school friends we trusted in possession
When matches were in session
With scuffed shoes, tangled laces
Ruddy complexioned faces
Pudding basin haircuts
No ifs, ands or buts
3-0 down at half time
Shock, horror, that's a crime
And the factory horns blared
Mum simply glared
Your defenders went missing
Come in now, the sun is glistening
Then fading light
Nothing to blight
That winger in full flight
Oh Joe, you should have scored

We've never abhorred
Your style, lightning turn of pace
But this is no foot race
Pass, Joe, give me that ball
You couldn't possibly stumble and fall
When fame and celebrity made its call
Against the Victorian wall
Over here, Joe, street poet
Lovely ball control, show it
Beat the scruffy keeper from there
On pavements, even stones
And old dog bones
With filthy school shirts
And girls with flirty skirts
We dropped our shoulders
Leapt over boulders
Beat the press
Nothing less
Five a sides
Above the fluctuating tides
Of late summer days
Tireless and evening greys
But come on, everybody
We'll play until dawn
On any lawn
Or patch of land
Once a bomb site, never bland
So, childhood street football
We fondly did recall

Our devoted sixties mate
Never a moment, you'll be late
No time to waste
More haste
Come on, Joe, double hat-trick
Please, you know you're slick.

MACCA AND LIVERPOOL

Now yesterday
Macca rolled back the years
To misty decades
Of 1960s' decadence
When excess and Beatlemania ruled the world
And Sir Paul McCartney was a young and fertile mind
With designs on greatness
But for a while
Did he pause for a while?
And consider the titanic legend of Bill Shankly
At animated Anfield
Where the seeds of the Liverpool revolution
Were planted like the red roses of yesteryear
And now
Ron Yeats was just impassable
Defensively impenetrable
A rock, hard and flinty
And Peter Thompson
The sorcerer, the conjuror
Flights of fancy
An elusive butterfly in the midst of thorns and bushes
A capricious soul
Who loved to tease, challenge and question
The accepted laws and practices
Of the winger's art
So did Macca consider
Last night

At magical Glastonbury
The wiles and styles
Of Ian St John, Ian Callaghan
Floating and flitting
Never a chameleon as such
Because Callaghan just obeyed his masterful instincts
And read the landscape of the 90-minute hoi polloi
With the studious eye of a Merseyside student
Swotting for an end of term architectural exam
Building original projects
Where the Kop sighed with pleasure
Just simplicity on his mind
So, maybe Macca
Intoned about getting things into his life
Or was simply content
To get back to where he belonged
Or maybe he was just amazed about Shanks
Drinking in the delightful beers and lagers of joyous adolescence
The heady fragrances of one First Division League title after another
A never ending conveyor belt
Of stunning prosperity on the pitch of green
Or maybe Macca thought
Of Bob Paisley, Joe Fagan
Waving arms, whistling through their teeth
Pleading, imploring
More hat-tricks please
Goals from all distances

Perhaps Lady Madonna was Paul McCartney's dream
signing
Where Madonna suddenly began to sound
Like the flawed genius of Argentine stock
Full of beefy, lissom movements like a gazelle
Flying across the pampas
Once ripping open Sir Bobby's England defence
With all the surgical ease
Of the obstetrician
Delicately moving the first operation
Or perhaps Sir Paul McCartney
Harboured the glorious ambition
Of just running over to the Kop
And assuring them that
Indeed
Things were getting better all the time.

ALBANIA'S FINEST AT WEST HAM?

Now here's the latest
On the incessant rumour mill
Albania's finest
But probably no relation to Norman Wisdom
Where he was worshipped like some cultural hero
West Ham now think their prayers have been answered
Armando Broja
For that is his name
But certainly not Mr Grimsdale
Where tomfoolery met the circus
Broja, Albanian but born in Slough
Reminiscent of Monty Python sketch
Most peculiar connection
Since when did Albania ever disturb football's global axis?
Little if any in the way of proven pedigree
Possibly comically
Inferior to the Germans, Italians
The French and the Brazilians
But let's give Armando the benefit of the doubt
Clearly better than some of his striking predecessors
Those who briefly travelled through the Stratford stratosphere
Poor and less than average
An East End concoction of ordinariness
Broja has been sainted at St Mary's

And highly commended at Chelsea
But Tuchel has no time for slouches
And those at Stamford Bridge
Who may not hit the ground running pronto
Not some point in the future
So it is that Broja could don
The claret and blue apparel
Where once the likes of Pop Robson, Clyde Best
David Swindlehurst, David Cross
Tony Cottee and Frank McAvennie
Fired goals for frivolity and fun
All conceivable artillery
And yet how did our honourable friend
From the land of Norman Wisdom's closest associates
Ever find his way
Into the innermost thoughts of West Ham?
The art of seduction can be so strangely powerful
David Moyes in desperate need
Of electrifying a forward line
Low on batteries
Broja, Dennis, Sarr, Simeone
Oh, how the Irons would love nothing better
Than to see Sir Geoff pulling on his boots
Emerging from happy retirement
This knight of the realm
Glorified and exalted
Since at this rate
West Ham may start next season in mid table
Before the first whistle

Or languishing in choppy waters
Near the bottom of the Premier League
Only six players needed
To give West Ham's season ballast without struggling
With the sharks and predators
Who just want to see them fall
Into a dark hole of inadequacy
Or just in the middle of nowhere
Thrashing around in obscurity
So, let those optimistic prognosticators consult the oracle
Maybe the Hammers will flirt
With those Premier League high fliers
Armando from Albania
Perfect alliteration
The stage could be yours
Norman Wisdom will be gazing down on you
With admiration in abundance
Don't trip over carpets
Where Her Majesty has tapped on your shoulders
Sir Norman now
With reverential kneel
But please let Broja become the knight in shining armour
Maybe a sir in years to come
When strikers wore
Claret and blue.

SUMMER

Summertime dreams
Lounging by lethargic sun beams
Football finds its transfer speculation
For constant illumination
Without expectation
Claret and blue anticipation
You have to be joking
Amidst the languid smoking
You scan the papers
For the shock headline makers
The intriguing rumours
But then the humours
Become stale and vapid
Just as the heartbeat became rapid
West Ham searching for Lingard, Sarr, Dennis and anybody willing
As long as we don't have to pay the shilling
Ward Prowse never douse the hopes
Those themes and tropes
Of yesterday, when Hammers revelled in their yearly holiday
Close season, your birthday
As the matches we fondly remembered
But then our hopes became dismembered
Buy as many players as you can
Before your face loses its tan
Once again it's City Manchester, of course

Let's cheer until we're hoarse
On the opening day of the new season
There can be no reason
West Ham meet Pep's Premier League winners
Those versatile plate spinners
In a class of their own
You can be sure there will be nobody out on loan
City will be looking for their hat-trick
Be sure they'll click
With clockwork precision
You'll be sure their decision
Will be right
And bright
At the moment there's only one more in the claret and blue fashion parade
Yet Hammers' bubbles will never fade
Aguerd in defence of the realm
Try not to overwhelm
Him at the helm of the London Stadium
As opposed to the Palladium
But now Mark Noble and skipper has retired
The midfield needs to be drastically rewired
A striker or centre forward they so desperately need
Somebody lithe and sprightly to feed
An assistant to Bowen and Antonio
In our portfolio
There has to be that elusive goal scorer
Without which we're considerably poorer
A Brazilian with the sublime genius of a Pele

Garrincha or even Carlos Alberto
Just for good measure
A national treasure
The happy Hammers now at leisure
Be prepared for August opening stages
And don't forget their wages
Those pampered Premier League stars
Foot loose in their fancy ostentatious cars
West Ham, now is the time to invest
In the best
Before we resume
And there's nobody in the room
With the class and technique
Of the unique
Splash the cash
But not before you clash
With ever pretty City
A joy and elation
An exquisite celebration
Surely not a third Premier League title, and words
Unheard of, again
When it's improbable
Perhaps within the realms of the probable
That successive hat-trick
That will really stick
In the craw
Of those we adore
West Ham, Premier League
New season, remodelled

Maybe mollycoddled
Exciting, biting, witty
And gritty
Come on, West Ham, your fanatical audience awaits again around us
At the London Stadium from the bus
As they assemble in their huge droves
From East End groves
Of learning, earning their keep
Gathering like sheep
Fans, fanzines, pies and chips
Where Docklands and ships
Once harboured our wishes
Amongst the shoals and fishes
Another season for the Hammers at Stratford's finest
Certainly not shyest
East London pride
Another shot narrowly wide
Come on, you Irons
No whines
Next season will be ours
For endless hours.

HUNGARY AND ENGLAND

Oh, go on
One more time
Before we shut up shop
And lock up until August
Football's temporary holiday home
Must have its place
In the wider scheme of things
We must hope
Tonight
Hungary will satisfy cravings
For more and more football
For some, a religion
Others, a harmless obsession
But even the Beautiful Game
Is in need of rest and recuperation
Not 24/7, every day, week, month and nanosecond
Of our breathing waking consciousness
Flashing and flickering
All the time
So Hungary tonight
And please FIFA and UEFA
You must be able to draw the line
Of course
Football must be allowed its moment
Of reflection and contemplation
Of last season's historic deeds
But Hungary has to be

The concluding chapter of the season
Remember instead
The virility and masculinity
Of Puskas, Czibor and Bozsik
Playing, toying, dragging
One way and then the other
Billy Wright's men on that distant day in 1953
When a misty November afternoon
Swallowed up English pride
Wembley engulfed
By Hungarian masterclass
England flattened 6-3
Magical Magyars
Memories of verve and virtuosity
Red Hungarian men
Playing with English standard bearers
Like rag dolls
Puppets on strings
Manipulated
And then locked in the darkest cupboard
Maybe they were marionettes
Who were just toys
But now 2022 and Hungary
No more humiliation, thrashings
A devastation of degradation
Rest, football, just for a while
Gareth Southgate
Enjoy summer
Please.

KEN ASTON: MY PRIMARY SCHOOL HEADMASTER

It's World Cup year
But this time at a time bizarrely close
To mince pie, turkey and brussels sprouts
Family gatherings and bibulous booze festivities
The wine of the day
The lager of the afternoon
Sandwiches curling
In meek acceptance of their fate
It was never too late for sleep
Dad and Uncle deep in the land of nod
That merry band who now dream the dream, snoring
Contented with their station in life
Amidst the fork and knife
But some of us remember
Our Ken
Ken Aston
A footballing man
In lung, heart, soul
Every fibre of his being
Always pleading for order
Ken Aston was the World Cup referee
Who rose above the chaos and consternation
When there was no need for complication
A towering gentleman through and through
Never blue

Mr Aston
For this football poet was our school headmaster
Never a newscaster
Presiding over Newbury Park
Not once did he bark
He was our primary school beacon of authority
A powerhouse of seniority
And yet when the pressure almost reached boiling point
And the world became a demon
Ken Aston stood apart from the intolerable burden
A wonderful human being
The man in black and the middle
A strenuous chore
When managers and players became a bore
He was unquestionably the man in charge
When Rattin threw his toys out of the pram
And Argentina were full of flim flam
Our Ken Aston became the official
For this was never beneficial
To the health of the 1966 World Cup
Rattin ordered off for an early bath
When tensions exploded onto another path
And then Sir Alf's blue bloods
Did indeed win, above the floods
Of sweat
Bobby Moore's young Lions
Wet behind the ears
Above the purgatory and tears

But victorious and only once
Sadly
Lest we forget four years before
In Santiago, Chile and Italy went to war
In the authentic Battle of Santiago
That day Ken Aston cut through
The bureaucratic mumbo jumbo
And took no prisoners
A World Cup referee supreme
Who'd taken enough
The rough and the tough
Stern and unyielding
The man in the middle
Charged over towards violent and combustible South America
Chile frozen in time, fuming
Now overheating, fists flying
Threatening blue murder with tempers of Latin intent
While the blue of Italy fought fire with fire
But never in the mire
My headmaster though intervened
In the nick of time
Game stopped, match over
Tall with splendid diplomacy
Then with raucous cheers in his ears
And the players had left the field
And the managers had expressed too far
You suddenly discovered that the World Cup referee
Had been comfortably ensconced in the school hall

Away from the chants
From football's joyous rants
On terraces ablaze with the fiery eruptions of hate
Never too late for vulgar outpourings
The outrageous scoldings
But hey, who cared?
Because Ken Aston was Newbury Park's primary school finest
Gleaming with integrity
Modesty at times
In all climes
He was the one who set up our lunchtime chess club
So caring and sensitive to parents and children alike
Listening and understanding
Like the Sunday vicar
Above the noisy bicker
And the jolly, comforting bike
Always charming over and over again
Over heather and glen
At school assemblies before yellowing hymn chants
He smiled radiantly before
You certainly knew the score
He would never deplore
Thank you, Ken Aston
Our headmaster from Ilford
Certainly not from Guildford
Born in Colchester
But he must have known Manchester
City and then United

When Sir Matt Busby led his sixties stars to victory
In the 1963 Cup Final against Leicester
Distinguished World Cup referee
Oh, what glee
Mr Aston, you were the best
Commanding over the rest.

THOMAS HARDY AND FOOTBALL

Now Thomas Hardy, 182 today
Hard to believe somehow
Time flies
But England's finest lyricist
Or word painter
Consummate novelist
Literary genius
You wonder which football ground, Dorset lad
Giving rise to suggestions
Of Hampshire, Pompey or Portsmouth
Naval connections
Once of Premier League heights
Rubbing shoulders with Manchester City
But Portsmouth scarf around his celebrated literary neck
Perhaps on first name terms
With Pep Guardiola
Or Jimmy Dickinson
Once a Pompey giant
Or maybe Hardy was a hardened Cherries' fan
Red and black Bournemouth allegiances
A regular at Dean Court
Or latterly the Vitality Stadium
Shaking the foundations of this slumbering corner
Of this Dorset beauty spot
Wessex in his blood
Or perhaps Hardy was a Saint of the Southampton parish

Where once Kevin Keegan
Mike Channon, Phil Bowyer
And Alan Ball plied their trade
At the cosy, snug Dell
Where goals rained down from all points of the
Hampshire compass
So, happy birthday, Thomas Hardy
Come on, Pompey, the Saints and the Cherries
Your cherished heroes
From terraces from far and wide
Hardy's poster boys
Your idols from long ago
Happy birthday, Thomas
You'll support them
For evermore.

FOREST BACK IN THE BIG TIME

Forest back in the big time
Where once Cloughie lorded it on high
Pacifist against QPR
When long ago
The League Cup threatened his tranquillity
But Cloughie rounded on
Violators with the wildest of flailing fists
Young man, you have transgressed
Never darken these corridors
At the City ground again
But Brian Clough knew purity when he saw it
And advocated the principles of terra firma
Football flowed
With the fluidity of the River Trent
Old First Division champions
Twice in a row
But at the end of the 1970s
When it seemed punk rebellion had burnt the midnight oil
And then broke out with riotous intentions
Forest were paragons of virtue
Liquid gold on grass
Passing of diamond
And yes, quite topically
Platinum with a lustre
Matchless and timeless
O'Hare, Mcgovern, Gemmill, Robertson

Francis, Burns, Lloyd, Birtles
Conductors with a thousand batons
Footballing engineering
Of the finest draughtsmanship
Then European Cup holders
Twice in succession
Miracles written in the finest handwriting
But Malmo and Hamburg knew their place
For Cloughie and Taylor
This was another day in the office
In boxes now exhausted
Go on, lads, you deserved the plaudits
Fulsome bouquets of lavish praise
Showered upon you again
But the City ground is alive again
But never really died
Nottingham Forest back in the big time
Soulful and delighted to be here.

THE LAST POST

Real Madrid 14, Liverpool 6
It was a privilege and pleasure
To watch you both
Footballing brilliance
Season complete
Thank you.

PARIS — CHAMPIONS LEAGUE FINAL

Ah yes
Amidst the boulevards and cafe au lait
Where the Champs-Elysees greets Champions League giants
Or European Cup leviathans
In the old money
Welcome to Paris
Be sure to savour croissants
At the Gare Du Nord
Liverpool are forthcoming
Imminent as the dawn
That cracks gently on European lawns
Manicured as your mind and soul
Liverpool, a wounded animal
After being pipped to the Premier League title
But FA Cup holders carved
In perpetuity
But Liverpool and Real Madrid
Footballing royalty
Embracing French romance
With almost 20 Champions League medals between them
A remarkable phenomenon
This is a meeting of kings
Liverpool still reminding you
Of that first dance
When Tommy Smith became the Roman emperor

And Mönchengladbach fell
Then toppled to the ground by KK
Kevin Keegan, fire and ferocity
Liverpool's first European Cup
It should always be that way
Rather than Champions League prizes to one and all
Since that's a misnomer
Just incomprehensible
The top four
Regarded as champions of their league
Oh, what piffle and nonsense
The Champions League Final
But City are the Premier League's champions
And market forces, Sky, BT Sport
Call the tune
Today's currency
The new money
What a palaver
Or maybe some of us
Are embittered by the absence
Of the BBC and Barry Davies
When the game was played on terrestrial screens
And you knew where you stood
But now no longer amongst European aristocracy
Where football only listens to its own voice
Of grasping avarice
The cash cow
Millions of Euros
Tills ringing in astronomical six or seven figures

But tonight the Champions League Final will be beamed by satellite
Another parallel universe
Some far away planet
Where the galaxy of stars will play in the white of the Bernabeu Madrid
So gloriously Real
Nothing fake at all
And Liverpool red and ready
To acknowledge their history
With record breaking achievements
It could be another night of nights
And, of course, it will undoubtedly be
Perhaps the spirit of Napoleon
Will touch the shoulders of Madrid and Liverpool
Footballing monarchs
Undoubtedly so.

THE CLOSE SEASON

Oh, the commotion and rumpus
It's the end of the season
And now the close season
Football in summer holiday mode
The empty void between high summer and early
autumn sooner this year
Since World Cup carnivals loom
Amidst the tinsel and glitter of festive Christmas revelries
How absurd, almost unseemly
But now the domestic season ends
With City as champs again
And Liverpool on the verge
Of yet another landmark Champions League trophy
How many will be that?
Almost a trophy cabinet
Amongst more trophy cabinets of silver
With only the mighty Real of Madrid in their way
Oh, trembling lips
Hearts suspended in readiness
For another open topped procession
Through the chatty murmurings of garrulous Anfield
streets
The neutrals are willing Liverpool onto victorious podiums
It could be theirs
And yet, now there is silence across football's playing fields
Broken only by barking dogs on far distant roads
Cross country trains now heading for the seaside proms

Rather than Old Trafford, Anfield, the Etihad
The Emirates and Spurs' new domain
A break, a hollow hiatus before the first day of August
When the Premier League's big boys stoke up the competitive fires
Normal service resumed
Referees' whistles hidden
In discreet corners of FA chests of drawers
Where none can argue their case for a while
Recreational goalposts and bars
In once atmospheric parks
Now reduced to empty green spaces
Of now white flannelled cricket summer splendour
Displaying their sedate finery
Next to white marquees
And dusty wickets amongst deep mid-wicket leisure and pleasure
Soaring sixes to different continents
And fours hooked over good natured drunken taverns
And third man boundary patrol
Football, though, takes a back seat
Nobody to mock, insult or vilify
Or even humiliate
Since essentially the fans love their targets of abuse
The opposition are hopeless
And always will be
The boo boys will always have the last word
But now it's summer

And football is just a memory from way back when
Now a Rothman's Yearbook page
Recording another season's highs and lows
Trials and tribulations
The kids will probably still play
On the pavements, the spacious grassy parks
Rush goalie, coats for goalposts
Scenery of timeless five a side exchanges
But football may not be the dominant force
Until August blows another round of whistles and jocular banter
But now football will turn
Into its familiar shop window of transfer gossip
Towards the rumour factory
Where thousands of South Americans, Africans
And obscure corners of Europe and America
Will hold out for at least 30 billion in the bank
And that's just for a week's work
Or maybe by the hour
The millions are non-negotiable
Yes, it's the 'Greed is Good' League
The great Brian Glanville was absolutely right
Anyway, let the bucket and spade brigade descend
On their exotic islands in the sun
Top up their leathery faces with tans
And massage weary egos and privileged accounts
The close season always seemed that peculiar moment when

The pre-season fixtures coincided neatly with
Wimbledon tennis
Strawberries and cream
The resounding clatter, thump and crack
Of the smaller ball variety
Football on its summer holiday again.

THE FINISHING LINE

After 38 editions of private teeth clenching
Month after month of emotional investment
The Premier League finishing line finds its final bend
The last chicane
The gallop to the post
It has indeed gone to the line
Neck and neck
City and Liverpool
Hard to choose
City would seem to hold the aces
And should burst through the tape
With adoring hymns ringing in their ears
For a moment, recalling another Bell
Sturdy, tireless, running himself into the ground
Colin, here, there and everywhere
Mike Summerbee, Rodney Marsh, Francis Lee
When football met Panini stickers
In a delightful rendezvous
Next to the Maine Road faithful
But today's City are more than upright citizens
More commanding lieutenants
Sergeant majors of today's platoon
Smartly attired men on the parade grounds
Of City's twenty-first century generation
Now the palette holders of today
Raheem Sterling
Still conjuring Jesus

Almost religious
But certainly a man with that mystical aura about him
Scoring goals and answering prayers
But then Merseyside could still be
The architects of their own triumph again
Like the artwork at the Sistine Chapel
Frescoes of timeless beauty
Heralds of future greatness
Since 18 old First Division titles
Remain impeccably beyond reproach
And finally one Premier League title to boot
Another flourish from the fountain pen
That underlined the Anfield signature
But Klopp can become the sainted one
Holier than thou
The figure of reverence
That Bill Shankly became
Worshipped by those who never stopped believing
In the wholesome ideals of past deeds
Faithful followers
Fidelity was never in doubt
Sadio Mane, Jordan Henderson
Virgil but not the one from Greek mythology
But a defender of some value, weight and substance
It could be the year of years
For Liverpool to snatch back their Premier League title
On solemn then sonorous Sunday homages to rousing
Jerusalem
The last page of the last chapter

What a pot boiler
A nine-month labour of love
The season ends on a conclusive percussive note
A thunderous crescendo
The last day of football's Maypole dance
Oh, Sunday, Sunday.

MARK NOBLE

Mark Noble, claret and blue
Through and through
Mr West Ham
Farewell for now
But you'll be back
You'll never lack
18 years at one club
Above the hubbub
It only seems like yesterday
But never grey
Dedicated and loyal
Almost royal
Happy to be here
Without a care
And forever in the glow
The game seemed to flow.

MERSEYSIDE GLORY

It's been 16 years since the red stars were aligned
When the Albert Dock flung open its blinds
Stretched and yawned
To the realisation that Liverpool had done it again
When Steven Gerrard fired a destructive rocket
Past Shaka Hislop the claret and blue custodian
From what felt like Swansea or perhaps Glamorgan
But Liverpool lifted the FA Cup
As once again yesterday
They walked together rather than alone
Cup winners again
Under the Wembley Arch
Shanks, Bob Paisley and Joe Fagan
Must have been giggling somewhere out there
Recognition of yet more legendary feats
This time Jurgen Klopp
Moved to the sensuality
Of the Anfield beat in North London
Thick black and grey beard
Alive and functioning
Face wreathed in smiles
Baseball cap perched aloft
Hair of pepper and salt
Liverpool fated to win the Cup
Since Chelsea were probably harking back to last year
The year before
And finally, for the third successive year

Heartbreak at the Bridge
But Tuchel's titans will know fonder memories
And brighter days again
And yet, defeat
Criminal negligence
To those in the Shed
Where once Chelsea hailed Roman
Rather than Caesar
European Champions
But not for much longer
Leicester and Arsenal
Cut the Blues down
In years gone by
When the mantle of royal purple seemed the perfect cut
From the kick off
Yesterday, when you could still hear the voices
Of Stans, Matthews and Mortensen
Calling out joyfully from 1953
When the world was in black and white
And TVs reminded you of goldfish bowls
And then when Alan Sunderland steered home the winner
for Arsenal
1979 Beaujolais
A geographical oxymoron
And Manchester United collapsed in the Wembley heat
Losing to the Gunners' cannon firing blanks
No Old Trafford heights
Then a year before
Roger Osborne bore no relation

To his distinguished uncle and playwright John
Oh, but we jest, Osborne
A Suffolk pint of refreshing lager
Ipswich within the warm embrace of the Wembley FA
Cup glory
Glory afternoon back catalogue
But yesterday
Liverpool found a Merseyside masterclass
A composition of beautifully written quavers and crotchets
Simple chords
Finely executed notes
Strings tuned to perfection
Choruses and verses, clear as a bell
Liver birds in excelsis
Movements in different keys
Tinkling the ivories again
Maybe Premier League winners again
Sooner rather than later
So, Chelsea
Chelsea is our name
And blue will be the colour
As opposed to yesterday's yellow
Rather like the splashes of primary colours and deep shadows
That preoccupied Wembley
In its deepest and most pensive thoughts yesterday
But then Mo Salah, Jordan Henderson
Sadio Mane, James Milner
The upstanding Virgil

Sitting like a rock bathing in pools of North London light
A monumental sight
Immovable, indestructible
Battening down the defensive hatches
A footballing anchor
Rather like Emlyn or Phil and Ron of yesteryear
Hughes, Thompson and Yeats
Just as impassable as London buses
In the heat of the weekly rush hour
Then Jordan Henderson
Immaculate as the Conception of the Anfield birth of
an era
That finally claimed the Premier League title
Oh Hosanna, Henderson
Approaching the autumn of his career
But still deeply in love of possession of a ball
Spraying passes like artistic graffiti
On the walls of London
Art Nouveau
Illustrations and carvings in Cup Final long ago repertoires
Liverpool in total command yesterday
For much of its duration
Then losing the baton in the second half
Jittery, sloppy and slovenly
Overcome by late evening stage fright
Nerves twanging like red elastic bands
Chelsea and Liverpool
Head-to-head ding dong
Flowing like Father Thames

Footballing Harlem Globetrotters
Nothing between them
A mini classic, thrillingly close
On Sheffield knife edge
In the second half, Chelsea show signs of vibrato
Vivacity in yellow
But far from jaundiced
Now energised and electrified
Reece James, Alonso
And the mightily impressive Thiago Silva
An ageless ornament
Clutching creaking bones at times
But then imprinting his reliable self onto the day's textbook
Finally, Kante enters proceedings
But even class simply can't tell
Mason Mount, so visionary and insightful
Looking around at Wembley like a sixth form academic
Drinking in the draught
Of its architectural magnificence
An England undergraduate
Now confidence gushing from the fountains of youth
Rudiger and Jorginho
Commanders in chief
On the top deck of this maritime beauty
Smooth as coffee on a Sunday morning
Then Chalobah and Kovacic
Pillars and columns in front of defence
Maintaining and caressing a football
Like men who were meant to win

But then found a red sea
Of biblical proportions
And finally penalty shoot outs
Hold the back page
Your breaths suspended like the high wire
Dramatic broadcasts
From electricity pylons
Finger biting exertions
Heads barely capable of taking in the immensity of it all
Tensions snapping
Then the Greek amphora of red wine
Tsimikas wins the Cup for Liverpool
Merseyside complete
Accomplished again.

THE PREMIER LEAGUE SEASON'S END

Not quite the end for the Premier League
Toilers and grafters
Silk weavers and sculptors
Clay and rock
Granite and gossamer
Oh, what a season
For claret and blue
Maturity complete
Four in the Fens
At forlorn Norwich
No more bumper crops for Canaries
Subdued by battle hardened West Ham
Sadly lost in that proverbial coalmine
Where only the defiant cries of last autumn can be salvaged
From the lonely loitering of Norfolk folk
Who can remember early season promise
But now back again in the Championship
It must feel like manure and peat
And burning ashes
Norwich's salad days will return
Permanently, they hope
When Dean Smith re-discovers
Bearings and pleasant feelings
Meanwhile at the top of the filthy wealthy Premier League
Manchester City's Arab sheikhs

Are hovering over gushing oil wells
Of glittering trophies
Another Premier League title
City yet to play as we speak
But Liverpool are gasping
In desperate need of oxygen and snookers
To overtake the relentless Etihad machine
Full of powerful pistons and pulleys
Liverpool held by Spurs
Now seemingly hitting a marathon wall
Anfield resigned to the worst
But no longer under the spiritual influence
Of Bob Paisley or Shanks
Or the generous Fagan, Joe of the Boot Room
All part of the Liverpool furniture
And yet, this season could go to the last tick of the clock
The final minute
Of a season of sumptuous sauces
Thick, lavish helpings of seconds on the last day
Final hurrahs
Nail biters and transistor radios
Down or up
Loyal fans barely able to look, understand or imagine the full impact
Tears of joy and happiness
This is football
Heavy with gripping emotion and pathos
Let's bring on Shakespeare
To score the glorious winner

From the subs' bench
Stratford Upon Avon's finest
Deep lying forward
Relegation or promotion
Terraces rocking and rolling
Burying heads
Or swarming onto the pitch
In their united overwhelming hundreds and thousands
Multitudes of moping melancholy
Broken by the strain
The gravy train
But then we congratulate those with promotion in their midst
So there could be palpitations
Shredded nerves
Spurs and Arsenal
Going head-to-head
Toe-to-toe
For Champions League Blue Riband contests
North London gloating rights
Inferior or superior
Two games to go
Local red-blooded animosities
Fierce, inflamed passions
Spurs gain a point
Now Arsenal still in full flight
A steamroller towards the finishing line
Arsenal gain the upper hand
Against lively, yet stumbling Leeds

Just about safe from the dreaded drop
But a team not entirely sure where the future may take them
The Foxes of Leicester
Creeping out into tentative spring sunlight
But devoured by ravenous Toffees of Everton
Who look at the sweet jars of survival
And chew delightedly at the scraps
Then the Bees of Brentford
Three more points
And honeycombs left behind by the Saints
Certainly not paragons of virtue
Season nosediving into nowhere
Southampton, just creditable
And nothing more
Wondering what exactly Mick Channon, David Peach
And the dearly beloved and much missed Bobby Stokes
Would have made of muddled predicaments
Near the bottom of the Premier League
Then quite sensationally
The dark, satanic mills of the Red Devils of Manchester
United
Plunge into hellish fires
At the seaside end of piers of Brighton
Who must have thought
The Punch and Judy show had come to the Amex Stadium
United thumped on the nose
Bleeding profusely with deeply hurt pride
Offended by their ordinary offerings this season
Burnley perched on the trapdoor

And at Turfmoor
Now fighting for their lives
Could Lowry still be on their side?
Amongst industrial bleakness
Factory gates clanking
Relegation cries out at clocking on for workaday duties
The dark smoke of demotion clings desperately to
grubby overalls
Of a season worn down by relegation
Clouds now hanging like white flags of surrender
Mike Jackson
Now no longer in charge of Thrillers
And probably Beat It anyway
Then Chelsea running on empty
Held by threatening Wolves
At the Bridge of Sighs
But nevertheless in the Champions League waiting rooms
Watford Hornets now sadly stung
By yet more Palace royalty
Demotion back to the lower dungeons
Of haunted Championship confinement
Roy Hodgson, a master tactician
But now retirement may well beckon
The Premier League
We'll miss you
When the final bugles are heard.

THE LAST EURO ADVENTURE

Oh, it grieves me to say
That claret and blue adventures have run their course
Stood the test of time
But no longer
West Ham fall at Europa League semi-final hurdle
That was memorable
And yet maybe again
Another day
Glad we were there
To see it all.

REAL MADRID AGAIN IN CHAMPIONS LEAGUE FINAL

Oh, that stirring rendition
Of Spanish melodies
From dulcet tones and voices
Real Madrid
The genuine article
For the umpteenth time
Grandees of European Cup history
And now back where they feel they belong
At the pinnacle
Shaking hands with the past
Back this time
In the Champions League Final
How many times now?
10, 11, 12, even 13?
Yes, definitely 13
Incredible, just incredible
But quite extraordinary
Defying mathematics and calculus
Logarithms and algorithms
Geometry and symmetry
A force of nature
Real Madrid
Exemplary ambassadors
On football's highest councils
Sitting on the lofty plinth
Elder statesmen of the game

Veterans of its inherent beauty
Frequent visitors to its banqueting suite
The gilded mirrors, the chaise longue
Next to the corner kick
Of the mighty Bernabeu
Free kicks taken next to the opulent ottoman
Next to the free kick
Where the referee's familiar spray
But not hair spray
Will dictate fates
And awaits breathlessly
It has to be emphasised
And yet
We remember the nobility
Of Di Stefano, Gento and Puskas
When Eintracht Frankfurt were crushed underfoot by
Real Madrid
A picture of devastation
Wreckage and carnage
The debris of 1960 in Glasgow
When 7-3 almost felt like business as usual
For these Spanish toreadors
Cape flashing the bull in desperate retreat
Barbaric by nature, were they not?
What a night that must have been
When you were but an apple in your parents' eyes
But Real Madrid were the pioneers
Before the rest became like trailblazers
Their football had mercilessness, cruelty

Indifference to convention
Because they did things that were unexpected
Unusual
Masters of art and forward thinking
Innovation
Formations that were neither diamond nor platinum
But certainly gold
Positions reeking of glorious improvisation
Switching and linking, hopping and skipping
To yet more mesmeric bossa novas
Passing with rich spices of oregano
Parsley and thyme
Flavoursome
Scented with yet more cinnamon
Passing that breath's sweet craftsmanship
And measured consideration
They must have thought
Real Madrid were just figments of our imagination
None could play in their ilk
But then the ball moved
Like a white tidal wave
Washing gently over our vision
And we'd just witnessed the greatest and finest
Unsurpassable
A dream come true
Football full of wit, joy
Remarkable surrealism
At times, classical instrumentation
And experimentation

Now Real Madrid will meet Liverpool
In the Champions League Final
All of our birthdays and anniversaries have come at once
Fitting dignitaries on this star spangled climax
To the European season
May will welcome Liverpool and Madrid
With warmth and tenderness so richly deserving
Of their rightful status and stature
Liverpool
Now many multiple winners
Of the European Cup
Bill Shankly, Bob Paisley and Joe Fagan will be watching
From a comfortable seat in heaven
Waving arms, pointing, whistling
Living every moment
Coaxing and cajoling, on their feet
Inspiring and exhorting
Pleading for that European Cup
Remembering Kenny Dalglish
Leaping over Wembley advertising hoardings
After Bruges had been beaten, fair and square
And finally Terry Mac, Ray Kennedy
Tommy Smith rising like a salmon
To head high into the net
Perfection again
Mönchengladbach in Rome
It was almost too easy
Steve Heighway danced the last waltz
With the Merseyside Kop

As opposed to the Spion
Real Madrid and Liverpool un the Champions League Final
It will seem like the ultimate outdoor concert under the stars
An exhibition of courtly grace under pressure
A rose garden of footballing mastery
Two stately galleons dropping anchor
Into the late spring dipping sun
Where Paris sighs admiringly again.

PREMIER LEAGUE END OF SEASON UPS AND DOWNS

It's the most spectacular finish
To any Premier League season
For quite a while
City and Liverpool
Like feuding neighbours
But high-spirited bonhomie
It is only a game after all
Jurgen Klopp's band of showboating Cavaliers
Certainly not Roundheads
Record breaking winners of the Premier League
Or First Division, whatever your interpretation
Only Manchester United on the same level
But Newcastle sailing in serenity of placid mid table safety
And yet, at the top of the Premier League
The Wild West warriors have galloped into town
With bourbon in their first thirsts
It's the Last Chance Saloon
For those in anguish at the bottom
And tremors of excitement in the furnace
Of Champions League and Europa League contention
Yee ha
We can hardly bare the ifs and buts
The complex permutations of it all
The trials and tribulations
The glowering disaster themes

The joyous coronations and crowns
The relegation and promotion soap operas
Managers with faces like thunder
Folding arms, jumping ecstatically up and down
Then running nervous fingers down the spine of survival
And champions elect Jurgen Klopp
Bearded and very pleased with life
On the Geordie coasts and peninsulas
Mo Salah still running at the speed of sound
Liverpool champing at the bit
It could be another season to remember at Anfield
Since Shanks and Bob Paisley are still gazing down
Judgmentally from the heavens
With analytical eyes
Pride bursting from chests that once took deep breaths
Then there's Manchester City
The other contenders
Overcoming the street entertainers
Who were once Marco Biesla's Leeds at Elland Road
Not entirely out of the muck and bullets
The grim spectre of relegation
The grisly and gruesome trench warfare at the bottom
Meanwhile Spurs repeat the 1961 FA Cup Final
When the first shades of greatness fell across White Hart Lane
When Blanchflower, Dyson, White
Mackay and Greaves
Were about to leave their golden footprints

Across the green industrial lands of one side of North London
Spurs get the better of Leicester
Who may still be lamenting the loss of Richard III
In Leicester car parks
And yet the Foxes crept out of the darkened Forests of anonymity
To win the Premier League
And now their season is safe
Noisy neighbours Arsenal and Spurs holding late night raves
Disputing territory, dancing the night away
Too many petty grudges
Recriminations galore
Post-match inquests
You'll have to resolve your differences
North London angst and altercation
Local derbies, full of needle, niggle
It still seems too baffling for anybody's comprehension
Yet as the Premier League fades into the night
Revelry unconfined
But indecision rules in North London yet
Turn down the raucous noise please
It's intolerable and unbearable at times
Some of us are trying to get some sleep
The volume is far too high
Those anguished acoustics
For those who may be dreaming of their day in the sun
Villa, for their part, are sailing into mid table serenity
The sun sinking on their season like a bronze gold medal

Steven Gerrard with a mischievous glint in his eye
He could present his childhood Liverpool
With another Premier League title at the conclusion
Of another tantalisingly brilliant and tumultuous season
This is proving far too much excitement
For those of a neutral position
Villa rubber stamping Norwich's relegation to the Championship
After all those rumbles of agricultural Norfolk combine harvesters
When the produce had so much nutritious potential
For the Carrow Road regulars
It all comes crashing down to earth again
For Delia and her upstanding and gastronomic chefs of quality
For Norwich simply can't make up their mind
Neither the top flight or the old Second Division
Tortured emotions for those of a yellow and green hue
What on earth would John Bond have made
Of this current production of under achievers
And woebegone souls who were never likely to be the stars
Of any Norwich future?
Oh, the crying shame
Southampton meet in similar circumstances
Where only the Palace can still stand
In royal detachment from the rest of the family
Who wave from the balcony
Trapped in the middle
Saints and Eagles

Comfortable allies in mid table mediocrity
Some of us are conditioned to that feeling
In the East End discussion rooms of West Ham
Where the light winds become ferocious gale forces
But not this year
Since Arsenal once again rule the roost over the Hammers
1980 Cup Finals are now sepia tinted documents
Rather like those sixteenth century maps of London
Of topical yesteryears
Barely visible landmarks
And now no more than a memory
Sad and woebegone
Hammers thinking of German battlefields of Frankfurt
Everton, still fighting for their lives
Doughty campaigners
Relegation unthinkable, of course
But the Goodison flames are still flickering
Remarkably, the Chelsea bandwagon stalled
Brought to a juddering halt
Tomas Tuchel's footballing tumblers
Acrobats and exhibitionists
No longer parading their sequins and frills
Not so much the dandies or fashionistas
More the trendsetters
Roman has gone
Empire ended by the greed and avarice
Of those who only thought of money and financial gain
And yet Chelsea, still on the hunt for Champions
League validation

And confirmation
Or certainly
Somewhere in Europe
Back in Hertfordshire
Where the sleepy suburbs can only wonder
When Watford will ever find their Premier League feet again
Demotion again to the Championship
Or seemingly so
Roy Hodgson fetching in spring sunglasses
The best of all coaches and motivators
But Watford are perhaps a bridge too far
Keep smiling, Roy
Wolves come unstuck against the seaside travellers of Brighton
Graham is very much an artistic Potter
And, of course, Manchester City
Financially influenced by Saudi affluence
Sultans of swing
And Premier League baubles
Yet again or maybe not
Leeds still teetering on relegation precipices
But maybe inspired
By memories of the Don
Don Revie
When football observers were polarised by their genius
Their flaws and foibles
Surely Elland Road, though, will breathe a sigh of relief
Come season's end

But Premier League fortunes can be so fickle
It's all very fingernail biting
A boiling pressure cooker of uncertainty and turmoil
The hot fires of tension
It could go to the final minute
Of the final whistle
Which is why football claims the rightful title
Of the Beautiful Game.

HAMMERS NEED ANOTHER EURO COMEBACK

For a moment you thought back
To the jubilation of 1976
When Sir Trev and Keith Robson were lavished with
triumphant garlands
Victory against Frankfurt
From the vintage claret and blue
When all seemed lost in Germany
So the wines could yet assume
An altogether sweeter piquancy
Grapes finely trodden
Allow the bottles to mature in the East End cellars
Ready to be poured down the discerning throats
Of West Ham's fervent traditionalists
Who were there on the night of 1976
When the Euro Cup Winners Cup was still a child
of nature
In your teenage pomp
Tonight though must have felt like German retribution
A lingering reminder of their genetic discipline
Sticklers for perfection
Fastidious in matters of attention to detail
You've always known
That German football can still remind you
Of their World Cup winning factory
Of fluency, correctness in their blood
Once again it might have been for West Ham

But sadly the Hammers were sadly lacking the cutting edge
The bludgeon and rapier
Behind after 51 seconds
Never really the team who overcame the French legions of Lyon
The story of their lives really
Claret and blue idealism
But then the harsh realism of defeat
In the first leg
Promising omens since
In 1976, the East Enders were narrowly trailing
From first leg escapades in Germany
So, maybe your visions of paradise may yet flourish
In brightly colourful eucalyptus
And the happy hibiscus of the vividly memorable night
46 years ago
When Keith Robson struck a lethal and stunning rocket at Upton Park
And Anderlecht awaited with Belgium lace and taffeta
Far too good for the East End troubadours
West Ham lose quite heartbreakingly in the final
Oh, the floods of tears
The fountain of lachrymose weeping
From tired, claret and blue eyelashes
Splashing down on the Green Street thoroughfares
In the Cup Winners Cup edition of the year
That preceded Britain's sultry, astonishing heatwave
That seemed to last forever
First though, Knauff shocks the London Stadium customers

Surely too early for panic
But then
As if by the wave of the magic wand
The home side scramble home
Equaliser from the human dynamo who has been
Antonio
Always available for comment and goal scoring
But then the second half arrived
And then the season's fading chapters seem to fizzle out
Into a less than dramatic denouement
The pages of this fairy tale now tattered and drained of energy
Oh, West Ham, it could have been your season to remember
Smudges of ink in the margins
But not entirely marginalised
Since Germany could yet be West Ham's Dunkirk
The Berlin wall fell
And maybe Frankfurt will yet feel the full force
Of the West Ham sting in the tail
Kamada looks as though the Germans have carved a niche
In Seville final
But you can never be sure
When there are fluctuating bubbles in the first week
of May
May yet be effervescent again
But your heart tells you that
That East End storytellers will not be able to their grandchildren

Of favourable fortunes in 2022
Still, a Euro trophy could be snatched from the jaws of defeat
But your gut feeling says no
Not this year
And yet we've been this way before
Keep the faith, West Ham.

PREMIER LEAGUE FINAL STAGES

Premier League final stages
Wow
This Premier League title race
Really does seem to be a delicious hot pot
Of intriguing stats and fine margins
A meat stew of succulent flavours
Gristle and bone, served with sauces and seasonings
Beef like butter in the salivating mouth
Too appetising for words
Destined to go to the wire
Liverpool and Manchester City
Locked in a tug of war
Pedigree thoroughbreds
Neither with a vice grip on the trophy
Since this could go down to the final Sunday
When the vicar will have to pass around the communion wafer
And take a half time break
The congregation must hold their breath
Even the stained-glass windows are becoming too steamed up
And dripping with condensation
The excitement, felt, touched, clutched
From the heart
The pews and the parishioners must have heard the Anfield roar

And the Etihad eruption of classic cacophony
Strike those cymbals
Bang the drum
A soaring symphony of wills, stamina
Chaotic colours, sounds of joy
The neutrals amongst us are revelling in these stunning sounds
A clap of thunder again in red and light blue skies
At the Emirates
Arsenal are back in the first-class economy suite
Of the Premier League's top six
Arteta's North London aristocrats are brushing up their etiquette
Observing all the protocols
Yesterday word perfect
Verbs and consonants, pronouns
Ralf Rangnick, caretaker in charge at Manchester United
But yesterday resembling a man with a mop and bucket
Who forgets to lock up the school gates
United, sadly going nowhere
And blasted into the North London orbit
Beaten comprehensively, thrashed
Out of sight
What on earth would Sir Alex
Make of this farcical charade?
This parody of United
A feeble caricature
Of Bestie, Law and Charlton
Dennis and Bobby gritting incensed teeth

Georgie might have left Old Trafford after half an hour
But the twenty-first century Emirates
Leaves modern United dumbfounded
Scrambled thoughts, where to go next
A goalless draw at Brentford
Thoughts turn to beaches and promenades
Where buckets, spades and tequilas in Mediterranean bars
Are being chilled to massaged players' egos
In Premier League end of season leisure centres of excellence
Spurs crowded out, stifled
Stopped in their tracks
Out of the running for Champions League tete-a-tetes
Meetings next season, perhaps
At the table of Real and Atletico Madrids
And the Milans of Inter and AC
But those discussion tables are still humming
Spurs are now in heavy traffic
Stuck in wars of attrition with noisy neighbours
The Gooners now in the driving seat
But none of us know where this journey may take us
Tottenham slipping on greasy poles
Realistically not,
The Bees had several jars of honey
Weeks ago
The season is now in its last throws of the dice
At the King Power
The Midland powerhouses of Leicester and Villa
Also settle for spring, sleepy and soporific
Goalless draw

If only they'd given them a mattress, a blanket and a cup of cocoa
Dullness, in dire need of a cup of espresso
The stimulus of the hair of the dog
The wake-up call of a black coffee
Spare us the indignity, Villa and Leicester
Of any more local derbies
Head for the warming, summer coasts
And, of course, City, a force of nature
Lithe as Olympic gymnasts
Supple of loose limbed movement
Flexible as trapeze artists
Always glorious, exquisite touch masters
Watford, just blown away in a gale of passing winds
That may now be resigned to another season in the Championship
Take five and take a bow, City
Finally, Norwich fens and farmlands
About to be swamped into the land of nowhere
Combine harvesters driving over yellow and green plots of land
Surely relegation but maybe Delia has some tasty recipes to warm the cockles
Heartening pies with plenty of gravy for the Carrow Road faithful
Resigned to the worst but their day will return.

GAZZA

Gazza
This is the cautionary tale of the man
Who fell into the deepest well
Amidst the sleazy debauchery
Of drugs, sex and rock and roll
Blurred visions of kebabs, lager
Growing larger
That took its severest toll
On the Paul Gascoigne of old and new
But we knew that this medieval court jester
Would always fester
In dark doorways of riotous hedonism
Nightclub tenancies where Gazza wined and dined
Drunk to the point of ludicrous forgetfulness the morning after
The thirstiness could never be quenched
This young genius could never be benched
So, the Geordie poster boy
From Newcastle's finest, but never coy
Oh, the impudence and insubordination
That Gazza gave us in spades
Upon the blades of green
Accurate and clean
Heavenly, angelic and ethereal skills
Gazza, passing of more refinement and yet more thrills
But then there was the World Cup of Italia '90
When Bobby Robson trusted his warrior but then crumpled

Rumpled with despair
When Gazza was booked and hooked
And Lineker winked and pointed the finger
As Gazza threatened to pull the trigger
Only for Waddle and Pearce to miss penalties that landed in Naples
A staple diet of agonising near misses
Hisses of English disapproval on Italian soil
Where the blood did boil
And then when Graham Taylor claimed not to like something
And questioned linesman on future employment prospects
Gazza in the midst of private turmoil
Grinning, gurning, gesticulating
Painting the town red, performing
Face contorting, burping and belching
To those who exposed his fault lines
When the wines once flowed
How dreadful it must have been living life to the full
But now open to ridicule
World Cup 1994 now lost forever
In the hellish realms of the nightmare goalless draw
Gazza had rebellion and non-conformity
Where none could find him in any dormitory
In that hard wired mindset
You bet
The party animal could never be tamed
And yet we never blamed

The excessive self-indulgence
In the beaming light of astonishing refulgence
Finally there was the Glen Hoddle fiasco of 1998
When Gazza sadly pressed the self-destruct button
Bloated and beaten, bloodied and bandaged
Paul Gascoigne, soul now destroyed
But spirit unscathed
Hoddle torn between the Gazza who might have been
A shadow of his former self
Now there's a tiresome cliche
Then Venners, Terry Venables and Euro '96
Oh, what bitterness and more tears and weary years
If only the lunging leg had connected
And affected our thoughts on 'Football Coming Home'
The Germans may have been weeping
Into their fulsome steins of Munich beerfests
Now Gazza though could only ponder
On days of lilywhite shirts of Spurs, Teesside Boro
And richly Scottish shortbread helpings of Glasgow Rangers
For now he has been cast into the land of isolation
Where once there was phenomenal popularity
Amongst the heaving masses
Gazza, you were the best amongst those in football
Who believed in the rest
Of his special talent.

DERBY, THE NEUTRALS FEEL FOR YOU

Oh woe, Derby County
Football fans feel for you tonight
Relegation to the third tier
The truth rammed home
Condemned to the darkest room
The lowest of lows
Sobbing skies over Pride Park
Cloughie would be livid
But fighting back the tears
'Fear not,' he would say
'Your day at the heights of football's princely plateau will return'
But for now the days of Dave Mackay and heady Saturdays
At the ground of the not so American baseball
Where once League titles flew the flag
For a while
Now dropping into what seems like a basement
Raich Carter, Bruce Rioch
Kevin Hector, Roy McFarland
Now ghostly names from the past
But one day, football will smile
On your tender terrain.

SEAN DYCHE SACKED AT BURNLEY

Here we go again
The sack race as opposed to youthful egg and spoon races
Sean Dyche
Now history for the Burnley bigwigs
At boardroom level
Sighs of discontent and then dismissed
In the blink of an eyelid
Relegation looms like an ugly blight on their landscape
After brief European dalliances
This season the wheels have fallen off
Brake pads need to be oiled
The engine is showing signs of rust
Wear and tear
And Championship sirens are wailing at Turfmoor
Burnley, a big club in the historical sense
Once revered by the Lowry appreciation society
League Champions from yesteryear
At the beginning of the 1960s
When everything swung in metronomic fashion
But now decaying and decomposing
Like a listed building that once housed captains of industry
But Sean Dyche with that gravelly delivery
Delivered straight from working men's clubs
In North West England
But now silenced
Is searching for another club with footballing crests

And distinctive badges of honour
Burnley
The club you recall from your 1970s burgeoning adolescence
With Ray Hankin up front
Leighton James shuffling, jinking
Dropping shoulders of footballing duplicity
A wing wizard
Head down poised like a cobra to spring forward
Pantherine, charging towards by lines
Feline pace, checking, baffling
Cleverness in his thought patterns
Cutting back onto his best feet
And crossing to the land of precise perfection
Both near and far post
Then Brian Flynn
Eager as a beaver
Plotting in conspiratorial fashion
But never a spy from the underworld
While Martin Dobson glided and pirouetted
A creative catalyst, a sparking plug
Casting a critical eye in midfield
Analysing the midfield like a surveyor of quality and taste
Spreading shrewdness and enlightenment
Over the Burnley skyline of the Lowry
Collection of pencil thin, charcoal industrial chimneys
And quaint mills of once mighty influence
Over clouds of smoke mushrooming over factory floors
Burnley they turned to on Saturday afternoons at three

Men, women and children gathered
For their perennial groans and triumphs
But now Sean Dyche
One of football's nice guys
Finds that managerial hardships are part and parcel of
our game
And yet sent packing
With vital matches to play for and points on the board
Surely, appalling timing
Grimy hands at the tiller
Perhaps misjudging their moment to make quite possibly
rash decisions
But Dyche gets the dismissive boot
Drop kicked into obscurity
Or temporarily, so one must hope
Burnley on a downward spiral
Will find just desserts
Time may or may not be on their side
But Sean Dyche has lost that much coveted watch
Your clock has lost its hour hand
And the cold door of farewell, Mr Dyche
Is this way rather than the other
Be sure to remember
If it's any consolation
Managers are always vulnerable, downtrodden figures
Never secure
Never sure of their place, their orientation
Always seeking the elusive chemical formula
For winning Leagues and Cups

Ruined and demoralised by their daily toil, drudgery
Victims of the game's changing moods and vagaries of climate
We know you'll be back, Sean
Born again
Gritty as granite
Leading from the front
And writer of more compositions
Essays of truth and sincerity
Long ball and directness
Or the beautiful passing game
On Brian Clough's well-cultivated grass
On the ground rather than aerial combat
Where football becomes a floating hot air balloon
Falling from the air
Like some intruder from another suburb, village or town
Sean Dyche, we wish you well
Since football managers could never tell when their time was up
Read the mind of your demanding owners
Football management
It has to be a mug's game.

HAMMERS IN EURO SEMI-FINAL

Hammers in Euro semi-final?
Can this really be happening?
A second instalment of 1976
West Ham, repeating history
Against Teutonic thoroughness
Eintracht Frankfurt
Pinch us before we awake to the realisation
That fate has reunited us
With our European Cup Winners Cup opponents of old
But this is the new currency
The German Euro rather than that daunting
Deutschmark
That always seemed to appreciate in value
Particularly when Bayern Munich were on song
And Franz Beckenbauer held court in his royal empire
For the German national team
A domineering and controlling giant of a player
A monolith of a centre half
But tonight the claret and blue toppled the team
That took its baton and cue from the current World
Champions
A stunning victory for East End
Vitality and dogged defiance
Squires of their manor
Country estate landowners
Of the London Stadium stately pile
A night to treasure in France

The natives will be more than restless
The Bastille has been conquered
No more days to celebrate
Savoir faire or Tour de France
Heroes and swaggering strollers
Lyon are ancient history
Dawson breaks down the French hysteria
And then finds a wall of Lyon silence
Their supporters open mouthed
Then Bowen finds another bull's-eye
And wins a caravan for his troubles
Super, smashing
But seriously these are rose complexioned days
Flair and fantasy incarnate
Claret and blue disbelief
Astonishment in eyes of those who can hardly believe
That 46 years after the night when Frankfurt came
To the Upton Park mud and divots
Sir Trev and Keith Robson with miracles in their feet
Would dismantle German hubris and presumption
Frankfurt beaten
But then
As if by magic
It came to pass that now Rice could be sprinkled
liberally and joyously
Over German centres of command
The shot of a man whose England credentials are set in stone
Another crucial goal
Oh, what a night

When the Irons found their way in France
To unlock the bolt of the Lyon Castle that may haunt
them for years to come
Surely, you're dreaming
West Ham in a European semi-final
Against a mirror image of '76
When Johnny was far from rotten
And punk screamed from its boisterous cot
Eintracht Frankfurt, surely not
Will somebody nudge the devoted hordes
Who follow through thick and thin
This could be our moment
In the claret and blue sun
Bubbles will never burst.

HAMMERS 1-1 AFTER EURO LEAGUE BATTLE ROYALE

Half time in Europa League
Battle royale
Quarter-final hanging by the slenderest cotton thread
For West Ham
The smell of the French revolution
Re-enacted in an East End stockade
Digging in the trenches
But Lyon at the height of French fashion
Jumping onto a Gallic passing carousel
A bewildering fairground
Of flashing, flickering lights
One-armed bandits of one touch and two touch
Spinning noughts and crosses
Lyon passing, handsome as the Palace of Versailles
But West Ham prepared for the French Post-
Impressionist arty Lyon students
A joyous lesson in neatness and precision
Rather like the most advanced engineering
Declan Rice, Tomas Soucek, Said Benrahma
And above all Jarred Bowen
Chivalrous knights in armour
Until Cresswell
Who stunned on Sunday against Everton
Gets his rudest of awakenings
Sent off when the mists of uncertainty hung heavy over
the London Stadium

Like cold blankets that fell abruptly across the East End
Like the early rains of spring
A chill air of foreboding lingers in Lyon next week
Yet even 10 men can still muster Dutch courage if that makes any sense
Bowen, still buoyant as ever, a winner
On Sunday and once again the back page headline grabber
A giant of a goal
Towering over the two-legged tie
Then a horrible dull thud and sinister sounding clump
When Dembele pulls back an equaliser from the precipice
When the French threatened to swarm
All over the Irons' battlements and ramparts
Crushing the Hammers with their proverbial French resistance
Now here's the story so far
Let's equip ourselves with stereotypical baguettes, appetising croissants
On cross ferry voyages across the Channel
Be prepared for Proustian lyricism
Wondrous passages of footballing grandiloquence
From the East End cradle of football
The arts and sciences
Of the Upton Park academy
Nicely cooked and ready to be served to the discerning followers
Of the West Ham way
Half time in the East End
And it could still be the right time for French cuisine

To be devoured with ravenous appetite
The Lyon main course
Drinking the finest Chablis
Oh, West Ham
You'll never disappoint us
Where the bubbles flight
Will be launched on next Thursday
On the night
You never know.

HAMMERS CHEW UP STICKIER TOFFEES

Now here's an ode to Everton
Perhaps a word or two of levity
Here's a phrase of clarity
Yesterday was 1980 all over again
It seemed much longer than years of ten
When Lampard senior danced
We were simply entranced
The dance of all dances at Elland Road
When full backs were allowed the luxury of the overload
Around that symbolic corner flag
Where the Upton Park wag
Giggled at diving headers
We'll drink joyfully at the Feathers
Saw the luminous light
Of the legendary night
Of the FA Cup semi-final
Wine for all
Of April boozy bacchanalia
Our claret and blue regalia
Victorious through champagne clouds of joy
We recognised the Everton ploy
And yet yesterday Lampard junior
May have been joshed and ridiculed
Just a miniscule
By Lampard senior
That'll teach you

For departing the claret and blue academy
Apparently
Still, he did have his halcyon days
Seemingly always at Chelsea
Inarguable back-to-back Premier League titles
When everything seemed so vital
Wine, song and Mourinho
Never slow to sneer into his beer
Some may call him the conceited one
But never Portuguese fun
Yet still he won
But yesterday Frank junior
Was your London Stadium revenge attack
For all those years of tears
Of loathing the Irons with your ironclad constitution
No more claret and blue jibes
Yesterday an absence of good vibes
My dear boy, a little respect for those who once nurtured you in the Upton Park nursery
On a modest bursary
At the halls of Upton Park
Learning and yearning for trophies
When Di Canio once pinched the ball off you
In the nine goal thriller against Bradford
Many years ago
Remember what goes around, comes around
Yesterday though, West Ham: immaculate
Almost as delectable as the Sunday roast
Raise a glass, a toast

With all the trimmings, chicken and stuffing
Nothing for the Toffees in a sticky mess
But still blessed
West Ham though
Workmanlike and business-like
But members of the blue collar union
Boiler suited, intensely conscientious
Never knowingly undercooked
Or overlooked
Just the right room temperature
On this stupendous adventure
Turn down the oven, Auntie
The sprouts and Yorkshire pudding
Have to be just right
West Ham, for their part correct
Pure, prim and puritanical
Lovely service, vicar
West Ham observe the Sunday psalms
Of late football season resonance
And they did
Aaron Cresswell curls a free kick beauty
That assumed a mind of its own
A bending, curling parabola
The ball seemed destined
To reach a distant postcode
But then flew past Jordan Pickford
Like a missile dipped in sweet marzipan
A goal suited for the artists' quarter in Piccadilly many years ago

More Monet and the Montparnasse
Than East End brush, paint, ink
And almost aerodynamic
Perfection in poetic form
But we of the claret and blue
Expect our fortnightly menu
Of Wordsworth and Keats
But briefly Everton draw level from Holgate
A shot to shock the jittery nerves
Of the claret and blue assembly before Bowen
Certainly not Jim
Because we knew what we could have won
Jarred, back in claret and blue
On the spot to tuck home winner
From Michal's muscular surge and shot
But Frank Lampard junior
Today was your nemesis
And this was the West Ham genesis
Of greater glories to come
On Thursday perhaps
When Lyon come calling
Surely not a shrug of Gallic indifference
French World Cup nonchalance will never do
The Hammers, once decorating the streets
Of Green Street and Barking Road
Get out the bunting and flags for all to see
It could be once again
Re-run the reel-to-reel tape, when
Festooned with fleet of feet

Were remarkably sweet
Cup Winners Cup triumph at Wembley in 1965
West Ham
This is your time, your moment
To create history in Stratford
Blow those April bubbles again
Everton, no show
But may escape the relegation trapdoor if only just again
But Frank, let's be Frank
You pulled rank
Not your day.

WORLD CUP DRAW

So, it's our cousins from across the pond
In World Cup combat
Uncle Sam, New York, New York, LA
Across wide expanses of freeway
Burger joints galore
It's America in November
For the gentleman whose waistcoat caught the masculine imagination
England against USA in the middle of oil rich deserts
Where once Peter O'Toole presided
Over windblown, huge acres of sand
In celluloid fantasies on the silver screen
Gareth Southgate in the Wild West
Surely geographically wrong
Southgate in Saudi Arabia
It almost sounds like the adventure T. E. Lawrence never completed
England also meet Iran
Where the wicked Ayatollah
Once brought blood, death, callousness
The dastardly deeds of a dictator's savage nightmares
To a country that never had any say
Helpless victims of violent circumstance
Ripping through and tearing up the rule books
Please peace prevail above mayhem
You then thought of the punctured heart
Of Ally Macleod when Scotland had nothing
But feebleness and capitulation

In 1978 World Cup demoralised days
Burying his ashen face in a sackcloth of ashes
A pitiful draw in Argentina
Scotland slinking off the world stage
And Peruvian wind chimes overwhelmed the tartan roar
Cubillas' thunderous free kick, the crucial blow
So, England are given the kindest or allegedly groups
It could have been far worse
Spain and Germany meeting in classic
A manifestation of epic minds
Football's mightiest imaginations
England then could meet their Home Counties allies
Scotland again
Possibly the fire and brimstone of the Welsh dragons
Or deeply emotionally, sensitively, Ukraine
A World Cup in winter awaits its Saudi hosts
The Canadian maple leaf
The Far East, mysterious tales of contests yet to be told
The Middle East
Biblical footballing scriptures in modern day incarnations
Europe and more global
Sweetest of confections
England, Gareth Southgate
World Cup questions
And positive outcomes
We must hope
56 years of wilderness wanderings
England
Bring home that Jules Rimet World Cup.

INTERNATIONAL FRIENDLIES

How to explain the significance
Of the international friendlies?
Identifiable as the week the Premier League relaxed its hold
On our thoughts and perceptions
Last night, Ivory Coast at
The Wembley cathedral of sound
England harvest three of the best
Voices gathered in unison
In patriotic England red, white and blue shades of jovial jingoism
Although not necessarily so
Since that would be too extreme
An overly emotive comment
Perhaps
Since the English love to see
Their white shirts soaked
With tributaries of sweat rushing
Cascading down from the terraces
Time for endless endeavours
Hugging the flanks
Tattooed tapestries of midfield passing
Weaving, stitching
Carving, nipping
Depicting illustrations of colour
Through Grealish, perhaps
Sterling, definitely
Since his relationship with Wembley has sentimental value

Brought up within the Arch
On vibrant council estates
He knows the geography
Of every blade of grass within Brent
Where Wembley Park tube train cries and whistles in tunnels
Where history still remembers the agony
Of the Euro 2020 Final defeat
To those Italian stallions
It still hurts
The second half kick in the metaphorical ribs
Pain etched on English faces
Like the lines of crumpled, yellowing parchment of old
On Saturday, England edged past the Swiss
Never a missed opportunity
To announce early World Cup bulletins
When the deserts of Qatar welcome the globe
Opening up new frontiers
When the richly extravagant talents
From the world's finest dining tables
Bring us Brazilian caviar
German varnished efficiency
Latin Argentinian tango, verve and salsa sensuality
Then last night, Ivory Coast
Reminded you of those nights
Under the Wembley lights
When the old stadium roared and growled in defiance
When Rattin once stormed off the pitch
Like the proverbial bear with a sore head

And the garden of fruition yielded green acres of 1966
fertility
Hurst, Moore and Peters
Hunt, Stiles and Charlton
Leaving gentle breezes of Jules Rimet Cup imagery
World champions once
But one day it will happen again
Fear not
Switzerland and Ivory Coast
Were amiable and placid visitors
To the White Cliffs of Dover
Nobody told us
Since you were much more concerned
With the gleeful, well-heralded arrival
Of our ten-week-old puppy, Barney
Not Rubble
He'll never play in claret and blue East End pulsating
dramas
But his left foot could take a mean free kick or corner
Or gently lob the keeper from the halfway line
And yet international friendlies
Barely acknowledged
In the heat of battle
Where Premier League trophies
Will shortly be born.

RUSSIAN EUROS? SURELY NOT

We must have thought it was an early April Fool's
My and wife and I must have been thinking
Russia, hosts for the Euros 2028?
Surely a mistake, a horrible lapse in judgment
Far too many shots of vodka
An alcoholic blur
Our imaginations twisted
By Russian fraud
The shocking audacity of it all
This is a deceitful sham
Roubles are changing hands
As we take in the chutzpah and cheek
After all the burning flames
Of hellish death
Fractured, broken Ukraine homes
Scarred and charred
Smoking, weeping Ukraine
And Russia looking to rub salt into the wounds
How dare they
In retrospect, there was the 2018 World Cup
And none batted an eyelid
In solemn Kremlin bureaucratic minefields
But Russia lose all perspective
On the cold fields of shame
Not hint of remorse or sorrow
Euros 2028, it's an ugly dystopian vision
Turn off the social media banter
Ignore the propaganda

It is the worst of all prospects
Let the subject never be mentioned again
Never even considered
Banned for eternity
Never spoken of, utterly taboo
Putin must be held to account
Before football becomes his childhood toy
His evil excuse for manipulation
Of the Beautiful Game
Russia, Euros 2028
Has to be a sickening thud on the grapevine of rumour
Just a subdued mutter and mumble
In UEFA's upper echelons
Where occasionally nonsense prevails
In potty, discordant notes
And voices of bumbling idiocy
International football in Russia
Now in the present tense?
You have to be kidding
After everything you've perpetrated, damaged and destroyed
Criminal violations of barbaric death and suffering
What a nerve
Putin, look at us in the face
Your search for credibility
Has just fallen into the darkest pit
A cesspit of disgraceful acts
Of unforgivable murder
Please, Russia
Just leave the Euros to those who know best
The air is thick with Putin's poisonous ways.

WEST HAM BEATEN IN LOCAL DERBY

Oh well, you can't always win them
Since the heady, dizzy euphoria
Of Europa League conquests over Sevilla
Brings claret and blue West Ham infantry
Plummeting down to earth
Spurs, yes, Spurs
It had to be their early springtime pageantry
Showing cherry blossom along the Seven Sisters Road
Tottenham
Parading their peacock plumage
Roses around the cottage
Spurs flaunting their North London feathers
Against their good-natured enemies
West Ham, admittedly on a high
After European expeditions
Still wearing their Sunday shirt and bow tie
Occasionally revealing their breeding and status
But then stumbling towards exhaustion
At the end
Benrahma volleys in his goal
But by now Spurs are in seventh heaven
Surely not Harry Kane again
But two up within minutes
Game, seemingly gone
Extinct, defunct, emphatic zero
Not a day for claret and blue jousting and sparring

Provoking Spurs into submission
But not today
Maybe a match too far
But no plausible excuses
Last Thursday must have felt
Like the equivalent of FA Cup Final days at Wembley
And yet the beauty of the game's art
Found chinks in the East End armour
Kinks, marginal deficiencies
Blowing hot and cold and then breathing heavily
Even Zouma and Dawson have off days at the office
When the photocopier refuses to work
Pens and pencils go missing
Taking early holidays to Costa sanctuaries
Perhaps rest your weary limbs, West Ham
Take a break
Don't forget the natty beach shirts and shorts
Garish displays of rainbow colours
Blending unmistakably into the Iberian Peninsula
Now though the Premier League settles down
For the Swiss at Wembley next week
Away from the chaotic jam of the domestic grind
Swiss rolls forward
Towards North London stages of friendly fire
But West Ham beaten by neighbours
Who never return cups of sugar and milk
Since the rivalry between Spurs and West Ham
Is a fiery furnace of bragging rights
Smouldering with the hot tar

Of local, gripping cut and thrust ferocity
Matchless and priceless
Spurs on another high though
Son Heung Min and Kane
Whose citizenship reminds the Hammers
Of a three goal salvo
Victory complete
But Spurs
Please leave the building quietly
Since you are nowhere near Europe
You win this squabble
But Lyon are not on your radar
Remember, Spurs
Look at the bigger picture
Touche.

WEST HAM — WHAT A TEAM

The stars were aligned
The moon was in the right position
Venus and Mercury were the perfect planets
Now football galaxies
And West Ham were through
To the last eight of the Europa League
It hardly seems possible
Everything was compatible
Symmetrically correct
You were here
They were there
The London Stadium
More Palladium
But without the revolving stage
Oh joyous, joyful nights of gold dust
None can surely overcome
Claret and blue fortresses
West Ham tip toeing daintily
Through Spanish lands of orange
Sevilla now reduced
To the sweetest tasting juice
It's been said
Over and over again
Sevilla, a classical victory
Carved out with delicate chisel
This could be the year of years
When the Hammers met their special rendezvous

Two matches
From a final collision with delectable fate
Anybody for Barcelona next?
Or shall we reserve judgment
One match at a time?
Then some of us noticed
Eintracht Frankfurt are back again
The 1976 coincidence
When the Hammers of Brooking, Lampard and Bonds
Obliterated the German advances
On a night of spectacular in so many triumphs
It was the semi-final of them all
Claret and blue of vintage maturity
With subtle hints of champagne fulfilment
Then Anderlecht was the last staging post
A match too far for your claret and blue
Woe and defeat
Still, last night
The East End conquistadors
Not Spanish
But hearty pie and mash diners
Satisfied as the grinning Cheshire cat
The Irons now made of steel
East End cockles and whelks
Over half time ruminations
Lavish helping of seconds
More gastronomic analogies
It would be stupid not to mention
Stomachs full of claret and blue

Splendour and hue
The rosiest complexion
Where fanfares and fantasies live
Then in the second half
The Irons consume with relish
Evenings of taste and discrimination
What a menu, what a victory
The finest and greatest of nights
At the Stratford empire of dreams
And the London Stadium
Decibels and speakers
Cranked up to full volume
It had to be Yarmolenko
The fans' darling poster boy
Music and poetry on our lips
Our Ukrainian warrior
Scoring the winner
And then the final
You never know
The complete vision
David Moyes
Remember the glow left behind
By Greenwood and Lyall
Then Ron and John
Thanks, but now
It could be your season of seasons, David Moyes.

CITY STILL TOP

City still top
City still on course
For back-to-back Premier League titles
Without even playing
Where Chelsea seem
To be playing Russian roulette
Where the stakes are high
And money dictates the market
The Roman empire is tumbling alarmingly
Or has fallen, quite dramatically
Beads of worry and agitation
In the Chelsea boardroom
They'll pay the bills
But not the transfer fees
Not even engaged in souvenirs and merchandise
In the land of Chelsea's commercial dealings
But Abramovich is now in the dock
Accused of dangerous liaisons with Putin
On the field though
Chelsea give resurgent Newcastle a rude awakening
But the Geordie bandwagon is rolling again
Relegation now but a distant yell
From Newcastle's tumbleweed season of haggard looks
Struggling at the wrong end of football's endless ladder
Neither up nor down
But Eddie Howe
Has inhaled the salubrious seaside scents of Bournemouth

And revivalist signs of dynamism are in the air
Still, Chelsea
Despite the state of limbo
Remain in contention for Champions League finish
Bruce Buck
Temporarily stills raging waters
Everton though are troubled
Concerned at dire predicaments
Beaten by the old gold of those howling Wolves
Everton cornered
In the thick tangle of forest that is the wrong end of the
Premier League
Lampard's dad
Who once jigged around a corner at Elland Road
In FA Cup glory days
Finds his son Frank junior grinning and bearing it
Goodison trapped in desperate straits
Surely not relegation for the Toffees
But who knows?
Leeds are leading the way
In relegation greasy and oily territory
Sliding towards the bottom
But Norwich now doomed and condemned
And facing the firing squad
Too late for any rallying or recovery
Oh, the Championship it has to be
Sadly, but again at St Mary's
The Saints were marching on
But were then stung by a hornets' nest

Roy Hodgson's football encyclopaedia
Once again gives Southampton a valuable lesson
An educated football mind
Cool and unruffled
Watford, stirring, emerging from the rough
Slowly but surely
But haunted by yellow shadows
Your Hammers
Riding on an emotional stallion
Yarmolenko gives his Ukrainian nation
Moving messages from the heart
A tearful acknowledgement of love and concern
Football thinks of its family and community
The claret and blue of East London
Give their negative claret and blue visitors a bloodied nose
Villains of the piece
So unlike a Steven Gerrard
Eleven of recent times
Villa, beaten and not so inviting
At the Emirates
The season is now bursting into early spring
Colours of red, stunning crimson
Arsenal, bolder and brighter
Football flowing
Like the endless silvery streams
That gush idyllically from heavenly heights
Football from a thousand art installations
Leicester outfoxed
Then finally

Manchester United, Liverpool and Brentford
All deliver from the good book of victory
Ronaldo, a hat-trick pass master
Outclassing Spurs
Blowing hot and cold
Conte bemused
But Spurs still in stick or twist mode
Brighton are rocking on their heels
Oh, if only Graham Greene were here
To pass honest judgment
Since Liverpool are pushing and prodding City
Professional at Brighton's rapidly fading season
Of mid table mediocrity
Brentford have been impressive debutants
Sipping from the Burnley claret
Confidently striding away
From quick sands of relegation blues
The runners and riders of the Premier League form teams
And not so fortunate
A Bayeux Tapestry of bruising battles
Spectacular light shows and fun fairs
Relegation and promotion
As many fluctuations of fortune and misfortune
As the stock market
Sinking hearts and soaring hopes
Football at its taunting and teasing best
It could finish on a high
Or hinging on the result you didn't want
High and low, precariously balanced

On the cliff
Or the Premier League trophy within your sight
Or the forgotten figures of yesterday's men
And condemned to an emptier world
But surely not.

MY DAD

You'll never know how much you mean to me, Dad
I loved you deeply and always will
And yet could never appreciate the visceral thrill
Although you never wore the football clothes
Of today and tomorrow's shows
At the feverish Cauldron of the Boleyn
Never moaning or groaning
But then
You said you couldn't stand football
So, I just sat down and contemplated
Never deflated
Your love
Permanently over and over again
At kitchen tables we discussed Mercedes, Jags
Your cigarettes and fags
But who cared?
Since when you walked through the family's door
And all things relating to the cars you did adore
But when I mentioned West Ham and England
Football's feet of clay
You simply closed the door on the topics of the day
Peter Lorimer's thunderous shot
So what, if Ron Harris tackled with fury?
You preferred Juke Box Jury
Football was just for muddied oafs and never the
discussion of the day
But you were the best, Dad, whichever way
It was Fulham even though

You went with the flow
Your acquaintance with the Cottagers
Had no relation to Bestie, Marsh or Johnny Haynes
You were simply content with snooker frames
I loved you, Dad, for you were the one
Your family thought you were glorious fun
Who, gently digesting Sunday sprouts
Questioned those football louts
Crunching Mum's lunch
Or brunch
You inquired at the necessity for the Big Match
When Brian Moore told us about the catch
Of the day
From Peter Mellor, Fulham's goalkeeper, home and away
Dad, you were the finest regardless of your aversion
To the football version
I knew without exception
Thank you for always being there, loving and clear
So affectionate and dear
Just my lifelong attachment to claret and blue
Upton Park, free kicks, corners, they were few
But you knew
My brother and I were there
And we cared passionately for you
I'll never forget you, Dad, because
You loved my brother and I unconditionally
Even despite the season
Though you could never identify
With Ron Greenwood, Don Revie and Sir Alf
Or that bloke Ralph from Spurs

At the passions and fashions of West Ham
And England when tanners became new pence
You must have known I could never sit on the fence
Dad, I knew you shuddered with apprehension
When the tension
Proved too much
But then the final whistle blew
And you sighed with relief
When Martin Chivers, Alan Clarke and Tony Currie
Finally took to the tunnel at the falling of the autumnal leaf
What was the point, you cried
Of 90 minutes of huff and puff
Men chasing a leather ball; all that nostalgic stuff
So, I hugged and embraced you, Dad
For I knew you were struggling with offside laws
How to keep the ball on floors
Of greenswards
Football of distinction
Co-ordination and the finest sheen
And that number nine who's now a has-been
I'll never forget you, Dad
Football was never your meat and potatoes
The flavour of any month
Though you must have had a hunch
But Fulham was your team although
You would never know
Or understand
Football's vocal band
When you crunched
Mum's adorable lunch

You hardly knew why football had to be so boring
But we understood your snoring
At goalless draws
On East End shores
Even when you began to cry
When the Eagles of Palace began to fly
But we would laugh together at the sudden moods
Of the day when the Hammers won with foods
In our stomach
The hunger for goals would never subside
We were never goal shy
Canaries, fly
But you were there for us, Dad
Always at our side you were
We knew you loathed the mention
Of football and its condescension
When the upper classes sniffed
At football's nonsensical riffs
You crunched Mum's lunch
At Mum's lovely brunch
And never disapproved of my West Ham colours
Of claret and blue covers
Of bubbles in the air
You were always there
Love you, Dad, forever.

This is my eulogy to my late and lovely dad.

WEST HAM IN EUROPE

Yet more European assignments
For the men in claret and blue
This time in the middle of orange groves
In succulent sweet Seville or Sevilla
The juiciest of ties
With little in the way of pips
But the narrowest defeat
Where a one goal deficit can be redeemed
And the London Stadium
Could be at its most melodious
Blowing bubbles in C Major
Or operatic arias, floating freely
From Westfield shopping centres
Perhaps the Barber of Seville
Cutting runs from Bowen
Not on duty
Last night injured
But still capable of weaving webs
The tie is evenly poised for West Ham though
The garden is still green
If goals can be found in East End shrubberies
And claret and blue bushes
West Ham, still emotionally involved
In Europa League conferences
Negotiating Spanish orchards
Of oranges, nectarines and tangerines
But Sevilla

Finely ripened last night
A goal to the good although privately dreading
The simmering pressure cooker
At the London Stadium
The Olympic Park
Ready to erupt again
As it once did
When Mo Farrah once kicked home
For Olympic gold
It could be a rewarding night
For those ironclad Hammers
Indestructible at times
Then leaky and porous as the kitchen sieve
But now hungry for more bountiful banquets
Feed Bowen, for Soucek
There can be a Czech mate
If West Ham can pilfer crucial pawns
Depose bishops
Remove kings
Vlasic though, still seems the wrong fit
A prickly thorn amongst early spring flowers
A Croatian calamity
In claret and blue
Benrahma's days in the East End possibly numbered
Unstoppable at times but not now
Darting and probing here and there
But uncomfortable, ungainly
The exit is that way, Said
But Declan was back wearing the purple robes

A crowning influence
Blocking Spanish channels of communication
Moving sensually and sinuously
Through the sunflowers of Sevilla
Gliding and sliding with effortless ease
Like the seasoned trouper years ahead of his time
Declan Rice, this is your stage
West Ham skipper for a while
But summer could bring richer pastures
At Stamford Bridge, Old Trafford, even the Etihad
Since multi-millions speak the most fluent of languages
With full stops and commas
He signs on the dotted line
Of Champions League football
Assuredly
But then there was last night
When Michail Antonio seemed
To have run a thousand marathons
Running for his life
But then finding leggy legs awkwardness at a Spanish siesta
Recalcitrant ankles
Pleading for sandy beaches
In the summer rum punch of Mediterranean warmth
Where buoyant Brits land the towels before the Germans
Claiming proprietorial rights
On those lovingly furnished sun beds
Where sun factor 57 dominates the footballer's mind
West Ham though, still in Europe
And ironically Spain

Where the toreador awaits
The London Stadium faithful brandish the cape
Ole West Ham
A paella for all
We can but hope they will
A dry red wine
Maybe a chianti
To celebrate Sevilla's fall
Dreamers will gather in the Stratford chill
Perhaps spring can yield
A claret and blue summer
To cherish a trophy to call their own
Let's wait and see.

PREMIER LEAGUE REVIEW

So, here we are
At the business end of the Premier League
City still
But only marginally
Ahead of the Merseyside cruiser
Liverpool
Edging nervously past the claret and blue marauding armies
West Ham beaten but unbowed
Liverpool, a study in pragmatism
Rather than the frills and thrills of days gone by
When Art Deco met Art Nouveau
Between the Shankly gates
Picturesque brush strokes
By Roger Hunt, Ian St John, Keegan and Toshack
A collaboration of gifted minds
Wired up telepathically and technically
Reading each other like weighty novels
Now Sane and Salah
Of sophisticated minds
West Ham unravelled
Like a red cotton reel
Sane nips in to score
Keeping Manchester City within arm's length
City now locked into a ferocious argument
With noisy neighbours United
Please can we have a little decorum, gentlemen?

It is only a derby
And you can have your ball back
When we tell you
Such unnecessary bickering and quarrelling
Meanwhile at Villa Park
Villa launch the cavalry and gorge themselves
On yet another mouth-watering haute cuisine of goals
Steven Gerrard is using his honours degree
And those rich Liverpool qualifications
Villa, heavily influenced
By Gerrard's Master of Arts
At the Anfield academy
Southampton hit for four
Then Chelsea
Blooming like an early daffodil
Ransack the Burnley vault
With a complete demolition job at Turfmoor
Surely within touching distance of top
Three or four will suffice
To be followed by dessert and pudding
At the top table of the Premier League elite
At Molineux
Billy Wright would have been horrified at the collapse
Of Wolves modern day icons
Who abandon their post
Yesterday at the hands of a Palace takeover
Where the flunkeys and servants helped themselves
To rich pickings

Patrick Viera's remembering his Arsenal studies and patient tuition
Under Wenger's scholarly influence
Now Viera gives us
A revolutionary era
And two goals at the Wolves
Mid table respectability
It's certain and definite
Then the Foxes of Leicester
Hunt in the way that predators do
Foraging and scavenging
Through the brittle fragility of Leeds
Now stripped of Bielsa
Who thought he had radical leanings
But sacked when over ambitious theories
Were rumbled by the humble
Of the Premier League great
Leicester back in the limelight
Top 10 finish without a doubt
Finally both Newcastle and Norwich
Almost gobbled up by relegation hounds
But paddling furiously against the drop
Eddie Howe's Geordie black and white stripes
Another pint of intoxication please, barman or woman
A rich foaming glass of victory over the Seagulls of Brighton
St James Park will survive the scars and ravages of battles
Against the fall back into the Championship
And finally, sadly, impending doom
Norwich City, unsure of their bearings

Neither good or bad
Too good for the Championship lower orders
But clearly unsuited for dinner jacketed gatherings
And champagne quaffing
At Premier League tables of gold but only silver cutlery
When Preston and Ipswich are visitors at another buffet
Brentford Bees full of honeyed intentions
This is their first time in the top flight
Debut season, wet behind the ears
But frightening the life of Canaries in a coalmine
Sliding back from whence they came
So refreshing to see
Christian Eriksen
Amongst the Brentford Nylons again.

FA CUP FIFTH ROUND

None could deny it was deserved
The Hammers were always far too reserved
Wembley and the FA Cup Final
No place for scandal or libel
A far-fetched claret and blue dream
Saints elevated as the perfect team
Angelic and anointed at a feverish St Mary's
Where the magic of the FA Cup told us quite clearly
Southampton were never the Canaries
The fifth round saw the Boro fan the fires of Cup shocks
Spurs always chasing against the regimented clocks
Spurs out of the Cup; not this year, Conte
Boro gave them the full monty
Tottenham's Teesside comeuppance
Out of the FA Cup for this year; above the wear and tear
Sadly, not the Cup too hard to bear
Simply not the coup
Besides the year simply doesn't end in two
So, Spurs move lavishly towards the Premier League heights
Concentrating on more realistic sights
But not top four places
Fit to tie the boot laces
Never Champions League contenders
May not even be pretenders
Surely not theirs by divine right
When the mood takes them; still vibrant though and bright
So, Liverpool, Chelsea and inevitably City cruise

Not in the mood for a quarter-final bruise
So, they sail towards the serenity of calmer seas
The FA Cup will never simply tease
For they are potential semi-finalists
Since either Jurgen, Tomas and Pep
Oh yes, Pep will give that talk
Walk the walk
Strolling with a supercilious strut
City were far too posh for Peterborough, but
Has the FA Cup more tomfoolery up its cunning sleeve
Where others could only give the Cup a mighty heave?
Or will City, Liverpool or Chelsea simply reign
Never ready to feign?
Because this is the semi-final, then the final
No room for mistakes
At the Wembley Arch
Forward go the Saints, pulsating and ready to march.

CHELSEA'S RUSSIAN REVOLUTION

Chelsea's Russian revolution
The Roman holiday is over
Abramovich hands the keys of oligarchy and wealthy properties
Over to the warm charitable trusts
The trustworthy hands of loving benevolence
Where now hangs the dark cloak of dictatorship
Rules with a rod of iron
Putin, choking the life force
From Russia without love
But Chelsea now deserted by the silent one
Who hides in the background
We can still hear the nasty orchestras of war
Discord in the air
And menacing undercurrents
Of sharp divisions over Stamford Bridge
Where once Premier League back to back titles were displayed
When the echoes of arrogance
Of the Mourinho regime
Sneered and snarled over the Bridge
And then later
At the incomparable Real Madrid
So it is that Abramovich retreats
To his voiceless bunker
Not quite a sinister force

For he still believes in the Chelsea of old and new
Trusting in his instincts as chairmen and owners do
But now the Russian bear
Will no longer be the growling, grizzly bear
Who sits on high at the Bridge
Pouring money and largesse
On this upwardly mobile fashion conscious West
London force
Chelsea bathing in their pool
Of their untouchable excellence
But gone now are the days
Of bulldozers and bankruptcy
Scrimping and saving for all their worth
Now Chelsea boast millions at the court of Abramovich
And yet he's gone
But still there in spirit
Slapping backs from the parallel universe of his world
Smiling with hirsute beard at his Chelsea
Blue is the colour
Mason Mount, Rudiger, Lukaku, Hudson Odoi
All on the crest of a wave
But carefully protected
From chaos and turbulence
Where Ray Wilkins once strutted the fandango
A bossa nova or two
Chelsea now in grave danger
Of losing sight of where they were
Destabilised for a while
But not quite
Because when Roman takes that holiday

On stunning yachts that float immaculately
But yet they continue to cheer
From prosperous highs
The Shed in peerless accord
And yet yesterday was a punch in the rib
A harsh reawakening of the truth
Oil reserves are not the answer for any of us
Waters dirtied, but tidal wave steady and clear
Ambition still there now
Who knows what the future may hold
For the good citizens of West London
Toasting the past and present
Still pretty chipper
But no longer in Manchester City's binoculars
Just panting and puffing in their slipstream
A team left behind
By the leading lights of the day
For Chelsea
The Champions League could still be their salvation
Their medicinal antidote
The perfect pick-me-up
A shot of something uplifting
While Ukraine fights for its life
On battlegrounds they never thought they'd know
And Roman takes a holiday while Chelsea bask in the glow
They will, they hope, conquer those below
Blue is the colour
And Chelsea is definitely our name.

FOOTBALL GROUNDS

There was a time at White Hart Lane
When those who thought they'd endured enough pain
But then came the Double
Which quelled the trouble
Back in yesterdays when
They gathered in force again
Rival
In survival
With North London foes
Then stepped on toes
Of Arsenal across the road
That less than amiable abode
Then Highbury yearned for trophies and titles galore
Without resorting to the goalless bore
Marbled halls and historic clocks
Perfectly suited to stylish socks
Mud-caked boots
And elegant suits
Gooners once and all
Classic exponents with medicine ball
Then Wenger stood imperious and tall
At Stamford Bridge where Chelsea remain perched
On the ridge of more cups and trophies
Not another set of selfies
But you remember the sand and mud
Of yesteryear's thud
And crunch

That motley bunch
Chopper Harris, Cooke, Wilkins
Osgood and Hutchinson
In charge of their manor
When the mood of the banner
Was "Blue is the Colour"
We once again discover
Chelsea remain the same name
Never plain, just vigorous, glorious, aflame
So, finally West Ham
Never a sham
Upton Park, a cathedral of good
Across the babbling brook next to the wood
Down country lanes
Where hope never wanes
Upton Park, that East End Fringe theatre
Where everything seemed much better
When the Chicken Run
Was so much fun
And we were taught the rudiments of football's innocent age
The game became beige
But then changed
Upton Park
Would never become dark
For the lights shone on claret and blue
Teasing, then the bubbles flew
Amongst soaring rooftops
Over commerce and shops
Where the East End display

Their splendid array
From football's tastiest menu
And then when we all said, 'See you
In 2016.' When the old
Had broken the mould
What taste
What a waste
The old ground we seemed to leave with too much haste
Our soul may have hankered
For yet another tankard
But Upton Park
Simply said, never in a million years
When the Boleyn was in tears of joy and elation
Near East Ham Station
So, London's grounds
Across hills and mounds
Where you can still hear the distant sounds of shuffling men
Who, from the old Den
From the daily grind
Never a bind
Loyal to the cause
Grounds where Eagles
Once we treasured
Rapturous applause
Without pause.

MANCHESTER CITY BEATEN

At long last
City have fallen on stony ground
Spurs
Their nemesis
Double completed giants
Reduced in size
No longer supreme
Liverpool and Chelsea
The title race is on
City shaken
But Spurs' blood
Pumping again.

DON'T STOP WEST HAM

Oh no, we knew this would happen
You feared the worst
That hunch
The crashing thump of premonition
An earth-shattering fall from visibility
Shattered shards
Of once colourful mosaic
Now no more
Than optical illusions
Where once there was gold
Now bronze would do nicely
West Ham
Fizzling out
And running out of steam
Claret and blue
Losing its fine bouquet
The grapes of pungent flavours
And vintage fragrances
Now turning ever so sour for the moment
Held to a draw
By Newcastle's relegation battlers
Defiant
Where before they might have been cowardly and submissive
Settling for second best
But not now
Since the Hammers have taken their pedal

Off their once streamlined motor
And the preposterous idea of a Champions League finish
Has been laughed and chuckled
Into some Hollywood studio factory
No more than some comical rumour
With nothing of any substance
That has any legal claim to reality
Just a charade
Of the farcical rumour
It was always destined to be
Craig Dawson
Planted a decisive lead
With a knowing head
But then the multi-millions
Of Newcastle's black and white vast aristocracy
Displayed the fulsome obscenity of wealth
Fraser but not Private from Dad's Army
Challenging the claret and blue battalions
With tireless scurrying
While Jo Shelvey
A native of East End charms
Essex in his blood
But now of Geordie accents and mannerisms
Stylish at times
With maybe a point to prove
West Ham in his heart
But never on his sleeve
Yet today was the day
The Hammers were dulled by thieving Magpies

Stealing the thunder and well-prepared script
Newcastle at peace with themselves
Clear as clarity itself in mind and thought
Liberated from apprehensive mindsets
Nervous as protagonists on the first night
Making sure that no more lines are fluffed
Eddie Howe
Who once brought bracing invigorating airs
To Bournemouth's seat of seaside education
Wears the Newcastle mantle
Time to roll up the sleeves
Of heavy industry
In those fanatical hordes
At the Gallowgate End
Where trophies are now demanded now
Tonight just before the News at Ten
Rather than some far off hinterland
Where only torrential monsoons of disappointment may lie ahead
Newcastle want now
Not the immediate future
No idle curiosities
Wild speculation
Just the Premier League trophy
With their tea and toast
On Sunday morning
Without fail
Black and white stripes
World domination

An immensity of Premier League frequency
Always kissing the Champions League Award ceremony
Winners always acclaimed and lionised
By kings, queens and prime ministers
Leaders of the free world
The greatest thing since sliced bread
For West Ham though
This is a moment of harsh, grating and metallic anti-climax
Of brooding, stuttering reflection
Just enough petrol in the tank
But surely no Champions League top four contenders
Content with more modest gifts
Rather than the rock of delusional grandiosity
Or stop the season
Now.

LIVERPOOL BEAT INTER MILAN

Ah, another special night for the Merseyside choirs
The liver birds in full song
Liverpool hit the highest notes again in keys of their liking
Last night, Inter Milan toppled from their mighty perch
Former European giants revered as the Italians
Who once spoilt an English summer
Last year in Euro 2020 final signatures
A perfect storm
And calligraphy writing on yet another page
Of Liverpool's highly esteemed document
Of the highest quality
When Roberto Mancini wore those fashion designer clothes
And England wept uncontrollably
Sobbing into a million glasses of indescribable misery
Ales of ailing misfortune
Then penalty fiasco
The cold Shoulder of shuddering defeat
But last night, Inter Milan
Once under the legendary ownership of Helenio Herrera
Fell helplessly at the feet of those star-spangled
Five-star, five times triumphant European Cup winners
Or Champions League, whatever your choice
Last night, it was Bobby Firmino
And the Egyptian wonder of Liverpool's global impact
Mohammad Salah who signed, underlined
Gave their ringing endorsement
To the gladiators of old

When Kevin Keegan, David Fairclough
Ian Callaghan, John Toshack, Terry Mac
Kenny Dalglish, Steve Heighway
And memorably Tommy Smith
Whose delicious meeting with his head
Set Liverpool forward to Roman roads
And the amphitheatre of victory
Against Borussia Mönchengladbach in 1977
When Liverpool and the European Cup
Became enduring allies
The one and only harmonious Mersey Beat
Where Gerry Marsden
Once sailed in pristine waters
And never walked alone
More like the vast congregation
Who once gathered in idolatrous mood
In Liverpool's glorious historic churches
Preaching the virtues of pass and move
And still do in the homely pews
Of Anfield's Sunday best, dearly beloved
Liverpool, serial conquerors on colossal nights in Europe
When Fairclough leapt like the proverbial salmon
From the subs' bench and lit up Merseyside
Like a thousand torches
While anthems hummed rhapsodically
From the adoring Kop
Tumbling, swaying, surging
At kick off, half time, full time
A mellifluous majesty of sound

Liverpool football club
United always
But not to be mistaken for Manchester
Now that would be sacrilege
So, Liverpool back to their finest strings and woodwind
Inter blown away by Jurgen Klopp's most perfectly tuned band of men
Immaculately hewn
Sensing the Champions League in their breaths
Wintry vapours left in their trail
Blustery winds of fortune here in dear old England
Storms of Dudley and Eunice
No, certainly not last night
Since Liverpool were sweeping their own inimitable brand
Football of pure and white as the driven snow
So beautiful and ready to show
You can almost hear the emperors of Shanks and Paisley
Bill and Bob composing their sweet ballads again and again
Pleased as Punch
Thrilled as the first dawn chorus
When everything seemed possible was achieved
And still is over and over again.

CITY AS SLICK AS EVER

Manchester City
Like a runaway train
Charging through the sylvan glades
The swaying curtains of the majestic countryside that is
Their Premier League journey
They remind you of passengers rushing to their railway
platform
Breathless
Before jumping onto the Manchester City Express
A locomotive
Pouring forth shining amethyst, topaz
The rubies of another Premier League trophy
Norwich had nothing to offer
But limp acceptance and resignation to their fate
The Championship
Rather like that old 78 vinyl record
That never lost its sentimental value
But then reverted back sadly
To a time when nostalgia was but a child
With bruised knees
And dirty faces
Football played in 1950s back roads and streets
Norwich
Wash and clean that sad and mournful face
And relive the good times
City now though
Stylish slickers

Unstoppable
As sprinting cheetahs
Stretching across the plains and open savannahs
12 points ahead of the once pace setters
Of August and September
When Liverpool and Chelsea
Must have felt like expectant parents
They'll have to wait though
For another day
For the re-birth
Of another Premier League crown
The laurels of triumph
Surely though
City had kinks
Flaws and delicate sensitivities
But here they are
Raheem Sterling, Phil Foden, Ilkay Gundogan
Pulling rabbits from their magical hats
Hypnotising and mesmerising
In equal measure
Scoring goals for fun
Like the sweet marzipan and profiteroles we once knew
in our younger years
Sterling scores another hat-trick
Again
The Premier League
Theirs for the taking
Let the inevitabilities begin
Take your bow

Now in the middle of the winter chaos of fixtures
And then the Bees of Brentford
Drawing blanks
In goalless bore
Against the Palace where banqueting tables
Of Patrick Viera's still reside
Richest furniture
Easy on the eye
As the chaise longue in the luxury of their world
Then Brighton strollers
Wandering by the briny seas
And enjoying their season of flights of fancy and fantasy
In the top 10
Neat and attractive
As the handwriting of the fountain pen
Inscribing letters
In the capable hands
Of West London hands
Christian Eriksen
So glad to see the Danish playmaker
Wearing the football shirt again
After the traumas of last summer
When the world's heart skipped a beat
And so too did Eriksen
But now emboldened
He's back in Brentford colours this time
Like some nobleman in red and white stripes
Then Everton
Out of any danger now

For a while
Since the wounded patient now looks so much healthier
After extensive surgery
Lampard's Toffees
Chew up
And then devour Leeds
Who continue to give us baroque and rococo
masterpieces
But relegation haunts them
Like a late night castle
Whom none should ever visit
Ghosts of their past still hovering in the dark
Oh, what on earth would the Leeds of Don Revie
And Billy Bremner have thought
In their wildest imaginings
There must have been a logic
In subbing Raphinha, a Brazilian genius
A perfect blend of coffee-scented, liquid ball control
Full of happy beans
Delightful skills
Now Roy Hodgson
Is back in football's higher dress circles
Amongst the yellow hornets
Of the Watford template
When Graham Taylor
Became the sainted one
At the Vicarage Road Rectory
Where the honeysuckle once lived in the shadow
Of the Luther Blissett and Ross Jenkins pomp

And finally Manchester United
Now words fail us
But this is not the classic novel and film
That sent us into lyrical raptures
United were held
By those Saints
Paragons of virtue
One Ralf and the other Ralph
Sharing common ground and philosophies
Of playing the game
The right and proper way
Moving the ball
Along the terra firma
Ground based assaults
Passes dripping with syrupy gold
Feet to feet
But revealing very little of substance
United
Dull as monochrome
No hint of any of the kaleidoscope of riotous colours
That once flowed from the boots
From Denis Law, George Best, Bobby Charlton
Princely presences
On once glistening green
Befitting of Saturday afternoons at three
Now sadly United boast Pogba
Brilliant on his day
But then moody and irascible at times
When evenings became darker and more dreary

Fernandes potentially untouchable
Whose beauty of touch
Soothes the hectic, fevered brow
Jadon Sancho so much to offer
Potentially a permanent England fixture
Jesse Lingard still in the red shirt
But for how much longer?
Marcus Rashford
We could go on
With pearls of praise and flattery
But for now
United are in dire need of an MOT
Beckham, Scholes
Giggs and Butt
Simply names
Vanishing into the brickwork of United's past
The Premier League
In mid-February
Ways of the world
Continue your play
On the greatest stage.

ILFORD FC

Suddenly the roar would go up
Ilford football club
Through the autumnal chills
The icy, wintry blasts
Of January morns of frost-bitten grasses
Coated with dew
But then
Those auspicious signs of spring
Where daisies and tulips would compete
In the early rounds of the FA Cup
Linking up the play
Always available in space
Passing with grace
To the manor born against Ilford FC
Yes, my local team
Ilford football club
Growing up in the leafy shadows
Of the Essex pastoral idyll
You distantly followed their progress
But then decided they were not for you
But you could quite clearly see
Quite visibly
The floodlights illuminating your soul
Ilford's floodlights beaming in the greyness of late afternoon
Where, joyfully
The late hustle and bustle of commuters
Home from their daily toils

Would converge on Lynn Road
Once the fabled football home of the 1948 Olympic Games
Where once Olympians stood tall
But once again
Leaning out from your youthful bedroom window
A muffled cheering would break the temporary silence
Of agonised sighs
Of despair reigned
And then rained
For a moment or two
No need to worry
When Ilford were still being held 0-0
By perhaps Canvey Island
You could only guess whom
Since the Isthmian League was that far distant land
That none would ever see
Since West Ham were your team
Of maestros and dancing minstrels
But fear not
They were your non-League cousins
With a lingering smile from afar
But Ilford played
Free from care and oppressive
Inhibition
Off the cuff
Improvising
When few must have known they were there
But we knew about the their valiant exploits
In the FA Vase Cup

Wembley once
Many moons ago
Doughty amateurs
With hearts as large as the terraced houses where we grew up
To see Ilford
Glorious on their day
But then
Withering and brown
As the leaves that fell on our town
Near Valentines Park
Where once James Brown felt good
And so did we
And yet Ilford football club
Are the proud denizens
Of Dagenham and Redbridge's new headquarters
Briefly rubbing shoulders
With the football League's lofty hierarchy
But Ilford FC
Over the neatly manicured back gardens
And indomitable sheds of our youth
Are no longer the non-League masters of their craft
When we were young
The fences, doors and window panes
Resound to a different melody today
Ilford's floodlights
In those midweek battles of yore and yesteryear
Where the cut and thrust
Of the Ley Street Lions

Would see off Canvey Island
Again
Quite comfortably
With something to spare
Oh, Ilford football club
Unbeatable and irrepressible
When the mood took them
We'll never forget you.

THE VOICE OF THE FA CUP

The voice of the FA Cup
Here it is again
The voice of the FA Cup
Baritone, shrill perhaps
Resonant as the tinkle
Of that long ago Rossi ice cream van
That once sated our children's tea time appetites
But the FA Cup
In all of its multi-flavoured layers
Cuts across the classes
From factory floor
To high tech office in the city
Football still has a soft spot
For the muddied heroes of Hereford
Now exactly 50 years ago
When Ronny Radford and Ricky George
In a sudden ambush on Geordie pride
Newcastle crushed and trodden on severely
The fourth round holds another treasure trove of images
Headline makers
Glory seekers
Diamonds of hope
Gingerly and neatly edging a step closer to that elusive
date in May
That magical page in our minds
Inscribed for posterity
Climbing the steps to lift the FA Cup
Perhaps for the first time

Or maybe again
This year
Kidderminster Harriers are hoping to be the carpetbaggers
Who steal the limelight against the bravura
Hammers
Thames Ironworks
In another age of industrial might
Kidderminster
Against your claret and blue warriors
Surely not Kidderminster
The carpet men will hand out a carpeting
To their foppish London aristocrats
Who trip the East End light fantastic
In Premier League gentlemen's clubs
Where the Garrick cigar elite
Quietly shuffle the Times
But the FA Cup will land on our shores
Through murky early evening light
Floodlights ready
To meet the darkness of four in the afternoon
February gala evenings
Where inquisitive souls
Seek solutions to the riddles of the day
Such as the winners of the first FA Cup
Insignificant perhaps
In the bigger picture
For today is the day
When the Cup brings everybody together
Over hedges, distant forests

And hundreds of miles of clogged motorways
Coaches ablaze with scarves
Rosettes again
Marching over the electricity pylons
Man United, Liverpool
Chelsea, Spurs, Leicester
Oh, and don't forget Boreham Wood
From Hertfordshire heartlands
Non-League
In smartest uniform
Always humble
Never ever likely to take anything for granted
Just delighted
To be amongst those
Who were accustomed to the Wembley way
And who made frequent pilgrimages
To the shrine of the 1966 spiritual home
Best wishes to the dreamers, the idealists, the wishful thinkers
Once Chesterfield and Plymouth were one match away
From the ultimate engagement
Of the FA Cup Final
Still
The patricians and magicians will shake hands for the cameras
And swop pennants of their glorious days in the sun
The FA Cup
It never fails to enchant
Again and again.

WHAT, NO FOOTBALL TOMORROW?

No football tomorrow
Football in a desolate wasteland
Of concrete worlds and hollow echoes of yesterday
The Premier League rests
Its aching ligaments, tendons
Ankles, legs and arms
Its wars and battles injured cruciates
Stilled, at bay
Mend those agonised sprains
The excruciating pain
Of the crunching tackle
That should have been a penalty
Not given
We'll never know why
Then recovery
Completely re-charged batteries
But still
The fans yearn to be amongst family and friends
The warm communality of it all
Where once the meat pie
Timed to coincide with half time pleasantries
Lively bon mots and bonhomie
Followed by thermoses of tea and contemplation
No football tomorrow though
It's unheard of
Unthinkable

None of those boyish, boisterous chants
Of terrace cheering
And bellowing salty compositions
Yet fondly sung
No VAR for this week at least
No referees with sprays
Where corner flags strike up lifelong alliances with goalposts
While cross bars wait for another day
In the wintry gloom
But who cares
We'll miss football
At Saturday lunchtime
Afternoon, a rarity
Almost an oddity
And then we conclude
Football will never be the same
Without its traditional continuity
So, we'll long for those hugged touchlines
The wing wizardry
That plucked heart strings across our dreamscapes
Of being at the match
With the people we love
So, tomorrow we'll scan the papers
For scraps and remnants
Of transfer gossip
Resounds endlessly
Interminable propaganda
But for Jesse Lingard

We'll roll out the carpet
For the West Ham parade around our streets
Sadly, though
Football without throat, noise
Volume or poise
Is a soundless chasm
Where nothing but stillness survives
Emptiness around terraces
That once shook with joy
Next weekend though
The FA Cup trundles into a million perspectives
The fourth round restores our faith
In football humanity
Since tomorrow
It's only speculation
And if only we'd played at home again
Victory would be ours
In our eyes and ears.

THE RAMS TAKE A BATTERING

Oh dear, Derby County
In danger of no bounty
Since those halcyon days when Cloughie and Taylor
were fierce and forthright
When the Rams were always in full flight
Today Derby are no longer residents of the Baseball Ground
Where gypsy curses were once found
In hidden corners of fulsome stands
Where once the exuberant masses witnessed the bands
Of pre-match Tannoy musical blasts
In 1972 and then the supporting casts
Three years hence
First Division League Championships won above the fence
Gemmill and Rioch occupied the middle domain
Engineers behind the machine and chain
Linking midfield thinkers
Who never had stinkers
Who remain in the hearts
Derby County
Where once Raich Carter
Once Bachelor of Arts
And then married to football
When Derby were a name to be reckoned with
His family who became wedded to fame
But now Derby
With Wayne Rooney in charge
Hover over the trapdoor of nowhere

Although they still keep the ball on the floor
But, Derby
We care for you in a compassionate way
May you recapture that day
When the penalty spot disappeared
And Manchester City were scared
Of those formidable white Derby shirts
Keep faith in the future where pride in your Park always lurks.

CITY — STILL FLYING

'Tis the last January
Of football's calendar month
A long way from the fanfares
Trophies, cups, baubles
And stirring deeds
The final acclaim
But City are flying
Vying for the feeling
Experienced over and over again
For the refrain
But not the rain of May
Where the princes in victory
Receive yet more confetti and confirmation
Of Premier League dominance
City, stopped quite suddenly
In their headlong charge for yet another title
So far ahead
Binoculars needed
To see the relentless gallop of the sleek steed
The horse kicking purposefully
For the final straight
Pep may be modest and self-effacing
But he knows the outcome of inevitabilities
It's written in so many stars
The Guardiola charm offensive is soothing
Cynical souls
Held at the Saints

But full of feints
Drops of shoulder
Clear the boulder
Now City bowl along
Switching gears rapidly
Fast fast, quick quick
Mesmeric staccato passes
Electric magnetic
A storm of magnificence
Streaks of lightning
Across St Mary's on Saturday
Full of Elgar's Pomp and Circumstance
Drums crashing on green turf
De Bruyne, Grealish
Full of fine lace and filigree
Patterned feet spraying crossfield and diagonal
Passes of sugar spun candy
Through the lines of complex mazes
Labyrinthine cul-de-sacs
For Manchester City
This is Manuel Pelligrini, Malcolm Allison
And Joe Mercer, revisited
Simplicity on a well-dressed plate
Of spices, herbs
Seasoned with mouth-watering designs
And multi-layered intricacy
City will be Premier League winners once again
Expression in their veins
Art in their heart

Painting from easels
From near and far
Or maybe not
Since Liverpool are still breathing down Chelsea's
London necks
Chasing, persevering
But not this year
Surely, their season is out of season
Since City and their trophy are waiting
For the royal command
Performance of champions again
It has to be theirs
Surely.

1966 AND ALL THAT

You must have been there
In 1966
When England saluted its finest men
Yeomen of the guard
Red was the colour
Patriotic to the bone
England, our England
In our homes
World Cup in their hands
But essentially
This momentous day
When Bobby was as blond
Graceful and grateful
As we were in victory
Despite the dramas and melodramas
But quite certainly
England had won the World Cup
When we were children of nature
Maybe once in a lifetime
But it will happen again
Quite emphatically
A reprise and repeat
Of circumstances and events
Poised to break into our world
Those simple gestures
Of spontaneous laps of honour
Dancing to the rhythmic beat of the sixties

Wembley alive and chic
With Bobby of Barking
West Ham to
His head, shoulders, knees, toes
And boots of hardy wear and tear
Genetically so smooth as butter
Composure for breakfast, tea and supper
Then Nobby
Teeth of impudent charm
Jigging for joy
Since the 3.20 at Sandown had also won
To make him fulfilled, satisfied
As well as Wembley 1966
Then there was Sir Martin Peters
Suave as a City gent
With pinstripe suit in stockbroker mode
Sir Geoff Hurst
Menacing as Denis
But gloriously aware
A genius in cloaks of claret and blue
Then, for country
His allegiance to national duty
In extra time
Of the afternoon's importance
Hat-trick
To underline his value
The significance of extra time stopping at tea time
Then, gasping
Tension sucked out of the North London air

Fingernails bitten to the quick
Over the line
Fine margins
But 4-2 commandingly
Russian linesman became English citizen
For that day of days
But we were still babes in arms
In the garden of home
Toying with the rich discoveries of life
Three, a deeply loved child
Nurtured in the warmth of doting parents
Who knew very little about the afternoon
Of history and heritage
Names reverberating
Like the chapel bells near the village green
Of cricket's evocative crack of willow
In July's dozing slumber
But football had given us this day
You were still far too young
To appreciate its smell, taste
And heavy with poignancy
A day to pass on
Anecdotes of Sir Alf's emotionless stance
Unsure of what to do on the final whistle
So, 1966 was never on your radar
But inwardly
You were thrilled in every nerve ending
And blood cell
But you were a kid in the midst of it all

Pretending that you too were imitations of Bobby
Geoff, Martin, Nobby, Roger
Excitable Alan Ball, with every reason
Then the Charltons
Brothers in arms
Jack slumped to the ground
Bobby cried buckets of tears
Falling on hills, fields, marshes
Dales and mountains
Of England's yesteryear today
But then
George Cohen, Ray Wilson
Emerged onto Kensington Hotel balconies
With timeless smiles
Acknowledging the cheers
On the spur of the moment
Before Roger Hunt led the historic procession
England World Cup winners in 1966
Perhaps yet again
In appointments of destiny
But for now
We can only dwell on that echoing delirium
Of penultimate July days
When you were childish detached observers
And waiting for literary pronouncements
From Ken Wolstenholme
Who declared the ultimate cry
'We've done it, 4-2'
Fans and all.

RAFA — SACKED AND NOT BACKED

Oh no, not again
Rafa sacked
And never backed
Everton
The club once known as the Bank of England
Give their marching orders
To the man who used to be
Rafa, the gentleman
With the bank manager aura
But surely not from Santander
Rafa
Immaculately dressed in formal waistcoat
But not ready for his customers
Not now, given the opportunity
For yet more emotional investments
Bankrupt of support
Robbed of capital
Since Everton are now back at the drawing board
Square one
After early blossom time
In the autumn of the season
Now Rafa Benitez
Victim of circumstances
Where once Howard Kendall, Joe Royle, Gordon Lee
And the stern and solemn countenance of fear
Drained, but not without care

Then Harry Catterick
Achieved the impossible
Sadly though
Never reacting to League Championships
From many moons ago
So, the Toffees had to chew on something much sweeter
When Harvey, Ball and Kendall
Were pulling strings
Of the blue symphony of life
And a cabaret of colour
And virile vitality
But Rafa has left via the tradesman's entrance
Where once trod Carlo Ancelotti
Goodison livid, furious
Revolting, uproar
From the other side of Merseyside
Where noisy neighbours Liverpool are still strutting, flouncing
Serial winners of the Premier League
And the old First Division
Everton were the team
Who might have been
Even if Rafa thought he could be the Spanish revolutionary
Who privately believed
He could turn blue to golden moments in the sun
Victorious again
But alas not

So, where do the Goodison Park residents' association go
from here?
Do they appoint some legendary name from the past
To salvage their season?
Or simply go around in ever-increasing circles
Taking consolation in Harry Catterick
Or Howard Kendall?
For they were witnesses
To the sparkling jewellery of cups and trophies
But Everton are in muddied waters
Sliding down tables
Of greasy, oily decline
Surely not relegation
It's unheard of
In the charismatic corridors of Goodison
Where once Bracewell, Sheedy and Reid
Waved the baton
And led the band with decorative flourishes
And goals galore
Sadly Everton are now stilled
Silenced
Wandering around in trances of grey
Rafa
The first to join the managerial sacking race
Rafa Benitez
We wish him well
But you were just the latest
Who never quite met the criteria

Of the Premier League standard
That demanded much more than you were ever capable of
Farewell, Rafa
But we'll see you again
Sooner rather than later
Surely.

BORIS: MORE RUGBY THAN FOOTBALL

Does the Prime Minister
Understand the finer nuances of football?
Its grammar and language
Its all-conquering vocabulary?
Boris, we know you're more of the oval rugby union type
But can you grasp the history, the ancestry
Of when you were an old Etonian?
Since they were the game's trailblazers
Pioneering FA Cup torch bearers
Forerunners of push and run
Pass and move
Deep lying inside forwards
The recognisable driving force of its origins
But Boris supports nobody but himself
Thinks of only him
Or maybe we've got it wrong
He voices his approval of Gareth Southgate's England
Because patriotism suits him down to the ground
But nobody knows
Whether Manchester City, Liverpool, Spurs, Chelsea or United
Make his weekend
Or indeed VAR is beyond his understanding
A hazy mist on his landscape
And then there was the indecipherable puzzle that is pressing
Free kick artistry

As illustrated yesterday
By James Ward Prowse
But probably not the Saints
So, Boris pins his colours to a London-centric mast
Chelsea, perhaps
Fashionable as the capital city
Wealth in every corner
Of Stamford Bridge, harbour, village
And the Russian chairman who never speaks to anyone
A voiceless presence
But Boris has much old Etonian eloquence in his possession
Stories of Latin but no sign of any knowledge
Of tracking back
Sitting deep
Hitting clinically on the break
Possibly Spurs
But then he questions
The instinctive push and run
Of Arthur Rowe and Bill Nick, yet
Boris, this was a team
Of arts and crafts
No need to wonder why
Or the claret and blue of West Ham
Purveyors of the '66 World Cup masterclass
England's finest hour
Moore, Hurst and Peters
It should be a school examination
An academic subject
As pleasing to the ear as the first robin when morning calls

So, Boris, please inform us in all your eccentricity
Whether your team plays through the lines
Or doesn't
Perhaps the practicalities of the game are more to your liking
Driving in crosses
The long, diagonal ball
That makes the fans swoon with delight
Get that ball into the box now
No hesitation
Boris, we need to know
Do you really follow
The Beautiful Game?

THE OLD DAYS AT UPTON PARK

In the old days
When we paid homage to the claret and blue
Amidst the stamp and clip-clop of the noble horses
Where the savoury perfume of hot dogs and hamburgers
Fell around our sensitive taste buds
Lingering for a while
Where the cacophony of ear-splitting shouting, yelling, blistering noises
Cut through the tone of the day
An uplifting concerto
Or maybe an overture
To West Ham at their most classical
The finished article
Glowing in technicolour
Upton Park
When a kindred spirit joined us together
For song and music
Where once our grandparents taught us so well
Then you gravitate towards the creaking turnstiles
Stubborn and moody at times
But then you settled into the plush accommodation
Of the South Bank terraces
Where the full time residents
Who paid their mortgage
To their season ticket duration
For years and decades
There can be no turning back now

So, you plant your arms
On the pristine claret and blue
The upholstery we'd always known
And suddenly the resounding blast of brass
Raucous, joyful trumpets and trombones
Blaring fruitfully along the Barking Road
Rather like our souls
We can hear them so clearly from afar
Come on, you Irons
In the distance, the tunnel
From which our heroes shortly emerge
For confrontations against opponents of steel
The band plays on
Towards a hearty conclusion
An hour before the first whistle of the referee
Then we glance thoughtfully around the tempest
And the overwhelming tumult of events of our times
Rumbling like the trains and buses
That transported our fondest wishes
On the match day of Saturday
We assumed it will always be that way
Engraved on our minds
Around the Upton Park pitch
Bags of monkey nuts
In sacks of snacks
For prodigious appetites
Meanwhile, men displaying their finest badges and scarves
Announce their declaration of intent
Slapping each other's back

With immediate gallows humour
Floods of joviality
Pouring from mouths of blue
But fear not
These are our friends
Our Saturday spiritual mates
Gatherings of similar claret and blue sentiments
Fretful and worried
Staring at pools of onions and ketchup
Haute cuisine
A gastronomic feast
Our days of wheat and yeast to keep our hopes at bay
Appetites satisfied
But prepared for now
So, on cold wintry November evenings
Sagas and fables
Left us broken and bereft
Stamping our feet for warmth
Then there was the fortnightly ritual
Of seething tribalism
Pushing, shoving, jostling
Huddling together
For security and intimacy
The South Bank surged forwards
Like banks of birds swarming for all their worth
A huge throng of vocal solidarity
Then voices perfectly oiled obscenities
Spurs or Chelsea were the subject of salty insults
Hate-filled vituperation

West Ham hated Spurs and Chelsea
And still do
But Upton Park was their Speakers' Corner
A place to express contemptuous and hostile chants
From the distance of years
Shivering and trembling down the ages
But still you can hear the midweek night matches of yestiyear
When the Chicken Run would greet the away side
Like sworn enemies in the heat of battle
Heads down
Away we go
And finally the floodlights
In North Bank unison and stylish synchronicity
Would yell from the rooftops
'We shall not be moved'.

THE FA CUP GIANT KILLERS AND THE HAMMERS

The fourth round of the FA Cup
A revelation of epic proportions
Perhaps an apparition
Possibly a figment of our imagination
But then credible
Viable
Anything that could happen did
That was unexpected
Once again the embodiment of our aspirations, dreams
Reinforced
The third round achieved the impossible
When somehow, it seemed mind-blowingly inconceivable
Cambridge, the university city
Presented us with footballing dons and undergraduates
And the River Cam flowed
With the sweetest selection of fruit and fondant fancies
But over the weekend
Cambridge stole the limelight
Like burglars on light feet
Sneaking through yawning windows
Grabbing the prolific booty
Scoring the only goal at St James Park
Where Newcastle have been gritting their teeth since 1955
For anything resembling success
Oh, the crying shame
Never mind, Newcastle

Surely not Hereford again
When 1972 seemed a horrendous scar on their top flight ambitions
Their day has to arrive
Sooner rather than later
For Gallowgate pride
Hearts still pounding away
There will always be next year
But Cambridge broke boundaries
Disobeyed the command of convention
Treading the black and white stripes
Into the lush green grass of the Geordie revolution
Now delayed since the wealth of rich Saudi money
Will speak the language of football's vernacular
Or the syntax, words, verbs and pronouns
That seem fitting the Newcastle way
A template of survival
From near certain relegation
That obvious blueprint
The policy of success
Only the Premier League will do
But first things first
Cambridge gave us a man called Ironside
And he turned on a sixpence or perhaps a shilling
Oh, it could have been a tanner but far too long ago
Now the fiver and shiny quid coin
Have tarnished the varnish
Of Eddie Howe's Newcastle rollercoaster journey
But a goal nonetheless

That stimulated the senses
Of the Cambridge Footlights
And now the comedy of any age
But still within the cloisters
While erudite students of the Beautiful Game
The splendour and beauty
That is etched into the game's historic manifesto
Of the Abbey Stadium's archive of fantasy
Now fulfilled
So, to Boreham Wood and Kidderminster Harriers
Also leading actors on fourth round night
Now Kidderminster once again meet
In the second instalment of the FA Cup's chapter and verse
When back in the hotbed of the 1990s
There was another cultural collision
With the West Ham art class
With its fingerprints of pedigree and stature firmly in place
But only a goal from Lee Chapman
Salvaged the Hammers' blushes
And then yet more tales and stirring stories
Of giant killing
Embarrassed in claret and blue
But not for the first time
And then Boreham Wood
Sounding quaint and rural
But never tedious
Hertfordshire's finest
But non-League's ambassadors and flag bearers
Representatives of the game's pulsing grassroots

Standards of decency
Through to the fourth round of the FA Cup
Oh, delicious nectar
Flights of fancy
And surely never amongst the favourites
To win the old trophy
But hope still springs eternal
Surely not in 2022 though
Wembley's honoured day of days
At Wembley in May
But Boreham Wood are the FA Cup's level playing ground
Just for a while
But no longer
When the fifth round beckons with teasing fingers
The bigger fishes will prosper
The pampered professionals
Who once travelled with us on our bus
But now speed past us in limousines or luxurious sports cars
As if oblivious of the class divide
But Boreham Wood
Kidderminster Harriers
And Cambridge United
Our glamorous personification
Of how the Cup used to be
And still is
No longer Tom Finney cigarette cards
Nor the devious shuffle and poetry of Sir Stanley Matthews
Blackpool's Tower of ballroom feet
But the Hammers will arrive in Kidderminster again

Freshly scrubbed
Ready to go
Prepared for their fate on the day
If only you could bottle the FA Cup's intoxicating brews
Of suspended belief
Then, that sumptuous day
In the middle of May
At the season's end
When trophies are delivered
When the cinnamon flavours of the FA Cup Final again.

FA CUP AGAIN — HAMMERS VS. LEEDS THIRD ROUND

West Ham against Leeds United
In the third round of the FA Cup
Still the one trophy
Where parched thirsts can never be satisfied
Since this is the one they crave
Hunger after
Like men in the desert
Seeking drops of water
Over the rainbow
Where the rains have washed away dreams
In winter's icy chill
But we'll believe that May
The FA Cup could be ours again
Now 42 years later
But not the summer of '42
So wicked and spiteful
It's a conspiracy
West Ham have never even so much as seen the chink of light
Away from the Wembley arches
Or underneath them
But over the weekend
The claret and blue men will dust themselves down
Again fondly recalling the hazy mists of 1980
When the Gunners were beaten fair and square
On the cusp of that warm May day

Early summer calling
When the sun rippled and shimmered
On claret and blue shields of honour
Bubbles effervescent
Witty East End badinage
Jokes and banners in full spate
Spreading around terraces of foolhardy wishful thinking
Then recognising that fate could be on our side
When the court jesters of medieval times
Danced on wobbly tables
Then North London's fair green acres
Awaited expectation on its front door
When the old Wembley wept with joy
For East End conquests of fear
But Leeds now stand in the way
Of another East End pub fuelled celebration
If only West Ham could witness
Another magisterial Sir Trevor Brooking
Parade of jewels
The header on knees
Seemingly falling back into fields of glory
The winner against Arsenal
Rather like the most graceful ballet
A stunning day
Now for Leeds though
The team once demolished
By a claret and blue bulldozer
When a wrecking ball smashed Don Revie's emerging, strolling swaggerers

In the nursery of their ebullient youth
Bremner, the tiger
With a snarl and customary bite
Lorimer
With a shot born of bloodthirsty ferocious feeling
A clap of thunder in the Upton Park midweek furnace
Then Johnny Giles
Swaying, gliding
In the gluepot of Upton Park
Could only sit back and admire
The Hammers' Seven
In the old League Cup
Its severity, its cruelty
The savagery of its power and direction
From remarkable distance
Unapologetic as the missile of fire
And so, West Ham go head-to-head with Leeds
Remembering the night of the Seven
When Sealey and Brabrook
Hurst and Peters
Carved for a living
The meat and then the bones
Of the decaying corpse that was Leeds
White as a sheet
Shocked to the core
Then traumatised on the final blast
Of the referee's whistle in the dark
But David Moyes will hope
That this year is his to savour

And revel in the victory
That always slipped tantalisingly away from him
At Preston's
Once Invincibles
Then the Bank of England of Everton
Found a currency of their own
But never under David Moyes
But then Manchester United
Summoned a successor to Sir Alex's paradise years
And found nothing but the charred remains and smoking debris
Of a burnt out United
On Sunday though
Moyes will assume an East End hue
Claret and blue
Fencing swords with Bielsa's Leeds Cavaliers
Certainly not Roundheads
Oh, what we'd give for another Stratford concert
Of resounding trombones
Tinkling of the ivories
Glistening guitars
Of an FA Cup encore
Yes, there was Sir Trevor's head in 1980
When Dev revved
Pike scampered like a terrier
And Pat Holland like a whippet
Hurrying here and there
To distances untold
Rolled down socks

With plenty to spare
Stamina personified
We can only hope that the bridge of 42 years will be
Not become that daunting journey from hell as well
So, let's just pull away from the platform
And the Cup will be ours
For John Lyall
Read David Moyes
A trophy in the London Stadium cabinet
We can only hope
You never know.

HORNETS STUNG BY THE HAMMERS

Within the space of two days
Contrasting shades and moods
Of claret and blue
On Boxing Day
The Saints were spreading virtue and goodwill
Then it all came unstuck
For the team once known as Thames Ironworks
Tumbled to defeat
To the Southampton chorale of saintly voices
Who sung for free on post-Christmas leftovers
Triumphing in East London skies
Of wintry chills
But returning naturally to snug homes in Solent
Bars of heady brews
Of winning away
But today
The Hammers found joyous afternoons
Across the Watford Gap
West Ham preached the gospel at Vicarage Road
But not the honeysuckle-scented rectory
Where Sunday sermons drift across the lush lands of Hertfordshire
Today, West Ham left behind their own victorious verses
Stronger than Watford
Who once boasted the grandeur
Of Ross Jenkins, Luther Blissett, Nigel Callaghan
And the peerless excellence of Graham Taylor

Defiantly long ball
But playing the game in
Some thought to be
Monochrome ways
Effective though
Punishing sleepy defences
Then Graham Taylor once led his England
And coached in his way
His mannerisms
But then in Holland and World Cup qualifiers
It all unravelled in grotesque circumstances
Channel 4
Controversially caught out his anger
Those sharp words of rebuke
And lecturing of linesmen
But Graham was fired up
A gentleman through and through
Galvanised
Ready to present his England team
Until World Cup 1994 became an American nightmare
No apple pie dreams in LA
Or New York skyscrapers
For Taylor's wandering minstrels
And yet today
Claudio Ranieri
Who once lifted the Premier League trophy for Leicester
Now finds himself in troubled corners and dark rooms
Sinister shadows of relegation
But if anybody can do it, Ranieri can
Slowly but surely

Watford will reveal their peacock feathers
And climb to safety
Today though
Soucek
Certainly no Czech mate
Benrahma
With velvety touches
Noble, ageless
From the penalty spot
And finally Vlasic
At the end
The rousing signature
Underlining the win in broad capitals
Amongst the Vicarage Road Hornets
The Irons settled the formalities
With the fourth
Those Hammers have ended the year
With their heads in the clouds
Dancing the foxtrot to the early dawn
Nothing won yet
But trust in David Moyes
For he was the one
Who turned everything around
When others thought not
Revolution incomplete
But labour of love
Work in progress
Claret and blue, be patient
It can still happen
We think.

WOE, WEST HAM, NEVER ON BOXING DAY

Oh woe, West Ham
Never on Boxing Day
Always seemingly the worse for wear
Under the influence of the demon drink
Far too many brandies
Or whiskies
Temptations of turkeys, again
But surely not
And yet
Beaten by the Saints
Just angelic, maybe
A paragon of virtue
Playing the harps of harmony
Far too many strings to their bow
Against the sloppy, slovenly negligence of the Hammers
For Southampton today
Read Boxing Day 1963
When punch drunk claret and blue
Consumed far too much claret for their good
Barmy incompetence
Lost 8-2 against Blackburn Rovers
Many decades before
Since the crown of the Premier League was theirs
Under Kenny Dalglish
Back then
Bryan Douglas, Andy McEvoy

And Fred Pickering
Plundered, looted and pillaged all before
At the muddy birthday cake of Upton Park
Eight, yes, eight
On the day 66 others
Billowed windswept nets
In the old First Division
But now West Ham
Hit a Boxing Day brick wall against Southampton
In a sense we should have known somehow
A horrible foreboding
The Irons should have been prepared
Rather like vigilant scouts
Looking over their shoulder
As opposed to blinking for just 90 minutes
Or simply not reading the writing on the wall
West Ham don't do Christmas
A team with a deep seated aversion to Boxing Day
For as long as we can remember
A loathing for end of year festivities
Forget it
Never even remotely interested
Now sixth and stuck
In that predictable rut
A predicament
That may feel like a kick in the ribs
That temporary standstill we hope
But 2022 beckons
And those who keep the faith

Now long for a winter of content
No more references to Boxing Day 1963
Simply a modest recovery
Simply mid table stability
Anything that resembles the West Ham
Of victories over Chelsea and Liverpool
And early season fruit picking
And glorious harvests
When August seemed to last until late autumn
And then the threshold of winter
But now tiring legs seek renewed vigour
Petrol in the proverbial tank
Another lease of life
Oh woe, West Ham
Please remember your August, September script
It was easily legible
A pleasure to watch
Replace the light bulb
Power on
Come on, West Ham
A renaissance for us all.

OUT OF THE CARABAO CUP, BUT WHO CARES?

The claret and blue regiment West Ham
With rather less in the way of footballing significance
Once again bundled out of the Carabao Cup
By the old enemy or
But still amusingly so
Spurs
From across the northern waters
Of London's geographical divide
Or the Littlewoods Cup
The Milk Cup, the Marks and Sparks
Poundland, Tesco, Morrisons Cup
Whatever your choice of commercial emporium
A product of our times
And still a highly valued marketable commodity around the world
But no longer associated with the old League Cup
Or perhaps that should read
The Alan Hardaker Cup
For he was the brainchild
The catalyst of this ludicrous anachronism
Out of date
No longer applicable to anything
As far as we may be concerned
Just a pointless trophy
With little to recommend to anybody in particular
Still the FA Cup's distant cousin
But not nearly as cherished

Rather like the consolation prize
And goldfish at the fair
But tonight
West Ham bade farewell to the League Cup
A meaningless reward
For hearty endeavours
And a place in Europe
We will certainly not lose any sleepless nights
It's a sham, an impostor, a fraud
Nothing to write home about
No more than a substitute for the real thing
A Wembley date in March
But still a trophy that may only be mentioned fleetingly
When the balance sheet at the end of the season
Registers your name
Carved for posterity
But lacking in value or recognition
By Premier League bourgeoisie
The upper classes sniff and sneer disdainfully
At its so called irrelevance
When compared to their lofty station
At the top of the Premier League
This, after all, was the Cup that began
With Rochdale in the final
When the sixties began to swing
But then Liverpool, Man United
City, Spurs and the big hitters
Brought perspective and reality to the table
And yet the Carabao Cup
It is a Thai energy drink

But intoxicating nonetheless
For all its critics and sceptics
An alcoholic incentive
A day for dizzy, giddy heights in springtime
For social gadabouts
And roustabouts
Well-oiled throats drink
From the foaming inebriation
In late March
A pint of your best
Be it Spurs, Arsenal or Chelsea
To lift that precious piece of silverware
Be sure that West Ham have more pressing engagements
Europa Leagues
And quite possibly
FA Cups to attend to
In the well-heated cauldrons
Of the Premier League's business end
The Hammers are modest guests at more important parties
Still impartial observers at the moment
Fifth on Boxing Day in the Premier League's highest tiers
A richly deserved position in the pecking order
A notable achievement
So far
But the League Cup still has some way to go
Before we acknowledge its place
In the hierarchical sun.

THE FIRST WORLD WAR FOOTBALL TRUCE

Paul McCartney once immortalised the conciliatory
shake of hands
When football reached the First World War truce
A sigh of rapprochement
Amidst the shrieking shells and bombs
The crashing, smashing, exploding pandemonium of it all
Screaming with fury
While the Germans and the English slowly
Wearily
Moved towards each other
In 'Pipes of Peace'
Paul McCartney smiled
And reached out the hand of pacifism
Then another shuddering jolt to the system
Before the mud caked medicine ball could be dropped
Into the muddy maelstrom
Thick, cloying acres of anonymity
The soldiers must have thought they'd never kick off
And just vanish into a misty land
Of death, pain, finality
But then it all came to life
Vibrantly so
The football match of them all
The one that signified the dignity of peace
Or a suggestion of being here and now
And so it came to be

That hundreds of men
Thick trench coated
Rifles and then boots on feet clung onto life
They meet on common ground
United by football
Kick off
Half time quite possibly
But no semblance of corners or free kicks
Simply the camaraderie of war torn men
Hellish scars of conflict
Stumbling towards the potentiality of friendship
Reconciled for a while
Love letters from sweethearts
From a Beatle's coat pocket
Then the match proceeds
With the white flag of spontaneity
Ball lands in perhaps neutral soil
Men gleefully kick the ball
In no particular direction
Soiled from head to foot
But moving
And then leaving their markers
Before turning on a sixpence
Quite literally
Shooting from another bunker
But this time on good, amicable terms
Hearts together playing for fun
But on Christmas Day
There were no dodgy debatable penalties

But the Germans and English playing in historic colours
No sparks of bitterness or rage
Just happy-go-lucky moods
Glad to be seen
On fields of mutual appreciation
Stop the fighting, feuding
The killing grounds
Where finally they saw reason and hope
An orange sun
No time to waste
Let's play the Beautiful Game
Because the world is
And always be so
Now let's see
The English can attack
With two sweepers to mop up at the back
Sweepers but not mine sweepers
They'll do even more damage
So, let the great Christmas Day match proceed
Without intervention from fussy, bossy referees
We know exactly how to play
In the warm embrace of sportsmanship
Let the game begin.

VIRUS CLAIMS FOOTBALL BEFORE CHRISTMAS

Oh, surely not again
History repeats itself agonisingly so
Football brought to a grinding halt by viruses
And a week before the festive jollities
Today football gazes into the hollow emptiness of
COVID-19
Or the moronic anagram
Stricken down by global despondency
Sickening
For somebody to wrap a sympathetic shoulder around its egos
The vanity project of TV exposure
But football downed by aching illness
Postponed for a while
But how long before the supporters
Begin to wail and groan their understandable displeasure
At bronchial or respiratory wheezes?
But this time it's Omicron
Oh, those antibodies have blocked goal scoring opportunities
Penalty box skirmishes
The rough and tumble
Only Leeds and Arsenal left
But this is a nostalgic leap
Back to the 1972 Cup Final
When Alan Clarke

Launched himself like a missile
Or perhaps a graceful swallow
Diving his header heroically past an Arsenal keeper
named Barnett
Not a million miles away from Highbury
But today the Premier League stares out of forlorn windows
Crying and whimpering at the desolation of the day
Terraces bereft of humanity
None of the consolations of highlights or repeats
On Match of the Day
Just pain and longing
To be amongst the community
Of scarves and outlandish banners
Programmes
Like holiday brochures
Literary goldmines
But we'll miss
Mo Salah, Raheem Sterling, Lukaku Pulisic
And even Citizen Kane
Spurs without Orson Wells
Perhaps fifteen times removed American cousin
Distant, but fondly remembered
These are the cogs and spark plugs
Of the Premier League
The lightning conductors
Goal scorers of breeding
From the grammar schools of football's seat of learning
Today though
They will huddle around the tinsel and baubles

Of their family Christmas glitter fest
Reflecting on what might have been
But then resigned to their fate
Because the race for the title is on
Could be closer than ever
A pulsating throb
Of the pulmonary glands
Excitement yet to be born
But today a stillness and quiet hangs like a grey blanket
Over St Mary's, the Etihad
Anfield, Goodison
Vast edifices of passionate attachment to the cause
Never failing in their support
Kindred spirits
Through thick and thin
No football today
But plenty of vocal contributions yet to be made
How we love life
And football.

FOOTBALL AT CHRISTMAS ALWAYS SEEMED TOO MUCH

It always seemed too much of a good thing
Unappetising, too heavy
After the mountainous helpings of turkey and sprouts
Just unpalatable
Particularly when your stomach felt
Like the washing machine you'd bought the day before
And yet there used to be football on Christmas Day
And the trains ran for free
And then in the winter of 1963
The old First Division developed indigestion
So, Grandma suggested Rennies
So, we gathered around only to discover
That there were 66 of the best goals in the land on
Boxing Day
Presents galore
Pampered we were
Honoured to be in the land of waterfalls and cascades of
goals
Washing over our living rooms
A drunken stupor that left us delirious with joy
Fulham score 10 against Ipswich
Blackburn indulge in East End feasts
Of cockles and whelks
At West Ham with 8 of the best
Liverpool demolish the Potteries of Stoke 6-1

And for all the world
It all seems as if the beers and ales
Of that festive day
Had blended with mince pies
And goals were raining down
From biblical heavens
And strikers with boots that weighed a ton
Were just involved in a goal scoring infatuation
With nets fit to burst
And they did as if for fun
When Coronation Street was simply in childhood
And the streets echoed to our game of football
Dribbling nonchalantly around lamp posts
And then laughing at the shots
That landed in distant shires and counties
Of England's green land
With an emphatic statement of youth
And regardless of age and class
We kept playing on Christmas Day
For everybody played football in festive moods
Tinsel on our Man United shirts
Turkey leftovers hiding in the red
Of Liverpool and Arsenal
Who cared about the supposed excesses of football over Christmas?
When moderation seemed the last of our thoughts
So, we rushed out to the pavements
Where once again

Amidst the thickening snow
We could be the Beckenbauer liberos of the future
Or Bobby in his imperious suit
But nobody worried about Christmas over football
For it was our game
For evermore.

CHELSEA – LEEDS: ANOTHER FIERY CONTEST

Chelsea – Leeds
Another fiery contest
Oh, Chelsea against Leeds
Shades of 1970
When the old Wembley Cup Final
Resembled a sand pit
Or was it an allotment site?
Where cabbages and radishes may well have been picked
By Billy Bremner or Norman 'Bites Yer Legs' Hunter
And Jack Charlton
Towered over the spectacle
Like the gentle giant who just loved a scrap
But then matters relating to the game
Were no agricultural thump into the stands
And yet 1970 was copied and photocopied
By the class of 2021
On the penultimate weekend
Before festive boots were trodden
No dubbin needed here
Just a blizzard of fists
Sweeping across impassioned lands
Where the Bridge met the well-educated feet
Of the Elland Road Bielsa ball purists
Brave and admirably schooled by a man
Who knows far more about the game's morals and principles

So, the final whistle went at Stamford Bridge
On the sabbath weekend
And all hell broke loose
The dam broke
Sheer bedlam
Rudiger, powerful
And yet, taking sport far too seriously for his good
Anger floods through his blood
Tributaries of fury
Pouring from torrential brows
Sweat on over-heated forehead
Then Mount, Harvitz or quite possibly Hudson Odoi
Joined the red blooded tempest
The hurricane of tempers
Bursting and boiling
Then we remembered
It was but a football match
Chelsea and Leeds
We've seen it all before
But no more animosity again
It is just a game
No more handbags
Please.

GOALLESS DRAW AT BURNLEY FOR THE HAMMERS

Oh, for the gnashing of teeth
Claret and blue meet in identical colours
Turfmoor torture, though
For the London Stadium academy
Where artistry and erudition
Remain the West Ham hallmark
But Burnley, they
At the heart of the game's history
The Industrial Revolution
When the belching smoke of chimneys
And Lowry's noisy factories
Joined forces with the striking cotton mills
Against charcoal skies
But today
Burnley ground out the hard metal
Of a goalless draw against the high fliers of East End
Who apparently should have won by a Lancashire country mile
So that nearby Bolton, Blackburn and Oldham
Should have heard the Bubbles refrain
Effervescent as the festive Jingle Bells
Roar from the assembled throng at the other end of Turfmoor
So, we settle for the point
Although it could have been more
Woe, but oh grateful for small mercies
But Burnley

No longer the irresistible force
Of Leighton James, Ray Hankin, Brian Flynn
And the sweet guile of Martin Dobson
Andy Lochhead
All bulldog spirit
Grit, greasy rags and oily cloths
That once painted a grey sky
Blue as the day when they once won the old First Division
With that famous 1960s year of sugar and spice
Of football from planets far away
Precise engineering
Without fault
But the Hammers are still fourth
With the right kind of tools, implements and instruments
Chisels and saws
That cut like butter through the Burnley brick wall
That simply dulled the threat
Of an East End foray
That might have poured its fragrant liquid
Into a pot of gold
That Burnley simply stopped at source
A blank day at Turfmoor
But if only the claret and blue of London's East End
Had soured the taste of claret
Of bullish Burnley
With its Lowry memories of old
March forward, West Ham.

MY GRANDPA JACK: WEST HAM SUPPORTER

What on earth would my grandpa have thought
Of this current generation?
The modern zeitgeist
West Ham through and through
Long suffering
Polish and polished
In the arts of following the game
From the objective safety of the grand armchair
With an antimacassar to cushion the blow
When the Hammers were beaten and overcome
As a barber with scissors
He would crimp, cut and chop the locks
Of Moore, Hurst and Peters
Bovington, Birkett, Dear
Redknapp, of course
With the studied attention to detail
Courtesy and politeness
With delicate fingers
Clippers oozing civility and propriety
In an age when short, back and sides were in vogue
And the mods met the rockers
If asked
Grandpa Jack would oblige anarchic skinheads
With a number four
Perhaps more
Then the dashing Mohicans would laugh at the absurdity

Of their sculpted scalp
Follicles like spiky cactuses relaxing in summer heat
But Grandpa Jack would smile warmly
At their arty expressions of the outrageous
But hey, it was the sixties
And Grandpa Jack would never object
To startling revelations
Of the new and different
He loved West Ham
Because they represented the underdog
Always locked in struggles
Against the ever present anxiety
Of the relegation trapdoor
And yet he might have re-assured us
That West Ham had won the World Cup
Indeed they had
When the end of July
Was his seminal moment
The barber knew best
Of infinite wisdom
That day
When Grandpa Jack quite properly put down
Brush, scissors and clippers
To acknowledge West Ham
Thanks, Grandpa Jack.

WORLD CUP — A YEAR AWAY NOW

Now confusion reigns over World Cup jamboree
A celebration of world football on its highest plinth
The summit of genius and greatness
Both former and now latter
But a year hence
They will gather in deserts
Of exotic sands and Saudi hospitality
But the World Cup
Near Christmas festivities
Seems like snow in July
Roses in November
Just weird incongruity
Not right
Inappropriate
Like some spiritual gathering
At the wrong time and place
But we will happily embrace
The breath-taking perfection of Brazil
Because their ancestors and contemporaries
Have kept the flame burning
One touch passing
And football taken from the honey pot
And nectar of foot loose and fancy flamboyance
Always welcome at football's most sacred tables
A force of nature
Shades of the master

Pele running through the blood cells of their DNA
Gorgeous impulses
Rather like the emeralds, rubies and diamonds we know so well
A natural phenomena
Almost supernatural at times
Then the Germans
Meticulous in their planning for any World Cup
No stone left unturned
Pedantic in the grammar of the game
Lethal finishers extraordinaire
Then the show off histrionics of Argentina
Part of the South American football's technicolour whirl and swirl
Of fabulous fairground
The Italians unpredictable
Hard as rocks
But a flowing exhibition of revolt and rebellion
A joy to be in their company
Then Spain
Also of recent gold dust
Full of the spirit of flamenco
The drama of the matador
Luring the bull into cunning traps
Cruelty perhaps
But daringly demonstrative
And then England
Always a riddle wrapped in an enigma
Not so much a mystery

More a model of exasperation
Not since 1966
Hurst, Peters and Moore
The holiest of trinities
Won the wretched thing
But only because Pickles rummaged
Through back garden bushes
And there it was
The gleaming bauble
Jules Rimet
The indisputable glistening gold trophy
The one the world seeks
With compass and map in hand
Desperate to be reunited
When England must have felt the reconciliation was beyond us
So, Gareth, please deliver this festive package
This time next year
Harry Kane knighted as Orson Wells
Citizen, freedom of England
Then Mason Mount, Declan Rice, Raheem Sterling in tandem
With ceremonial gusto
Then Jadon Sancho
And Harry of Manchester United
Robes of red
But now patriotically appointed
Grealish, reminiscent of Gazza
But without the belching at airports

The comic posturings
Grealish
Bandy legged and beguiling
Ball control at close quarters
Art at so many levels
So, next year
The World Cup will find us overwhelmed
By heavenly skills from the Olympian heights
The epitome of elegance
From the ballrooms and penthouse suites of world football
From football's most pampered feet
Where the wealthiest ambassadors from FIFA
Will keep the World Cup
And its history
In flourishing health.

FA CUP SECOND ROUND AGAIN

Ah, there goes the clarion call again
The FA Cup juggernaut shudders into vibrant life
The supermarket workers and milkmen
Stirred by the morning call
Of the FA Cup charabanc of old, rusting coaches
Their precious day in the limelight
Both Yeovil who have had previous dalliances with the
FA Cup
Are back in the third round, again
Cider and scrumpy first orders night
Toasting Somerset's finest with glasses
Of foaming fuel of alcoholic heaven
And Morecambe as well
If only Eric knew of how his team had fared
But Eric followed Luton
But then his hometown Morecambe toppled Buxton
Whose purest waters are now no longer flowing
Through the streams of our lives
But Morecambe are through to the third round
Oh, the FA Cup and its level playing ground
Its sense of equality
Where the part timers of humble stations in life
Just to feel the distant scent
Of Wembley in their breaths
Then the labourers, the builders
The hod carriers with muscles like boulders
Carry the burden of those little market towns

Where the unknown teams from the highest mountain tops
Trundle out of the tunnel
Dim lights from swaying trees
Then the fragile floodlights increase their hold and power
On the FA Cup
Their day in the infant days of winter
When the gusts and gales
Of the teasing, capricious Cup glories of the FA Cup
second round
Blow playfully
So close to the back pages of history tomorrow
Giant killers
Teams from way out in Middle England
Or close to suburbia
Threaten the bigger boys in the playground
Yeovil against Manchester City
It surely will never happen at the third round rendezvous
Where the interlopers and the modestly ambitious
Yell from the highest steeples
Hoping that David will slay Goliath
And the world will keep turning
Oh, the FA Cup.

RAY KENNEDY

For those who were not of a red persuasion
Be it Liverpool or Arsenal
Ray Kennedy decorated the Beautiful Game
With ornate patterns
Embellished with rich textures of class and style
A style icon
Sadly though
Ray Kennedy
Of the parish of Highbury and Anfield
Died today, nobly
Majestically adorning the seats of learning
Of football's finest theatres and galleries
Our Ray, cultured feet
So visionary and radical in his thinking
Seeing by far the bigger picture
The wider scheme of things
Constantly imagining perceptive angles
A model of trigonometry on a football pitch
Now there's a thought
When Charlie George and George Graham
Carved vivid images at Highbury
And Kenny Dalglish fed on a substantial diet
Of goals from the Kennedy wand of sorcery
Then England came calling
And, of course, our Ray was the metronome
Swinging metrically perfect passes
Into fecund and feverish penalty areas

Guiding the ball
Cajoling and coaxing it
Breathing life and encouragement into the birth of a game
The quiet man, the unfussy man
A man of huge footballing intellect
Towering above the rest
With that ever present air of upper-class refinement
A player of cultivated bearing
A conductor of all orchestral themes
Farewell, Ray Kennedy
Thank you, our friend.

WHAT WOULD PETER JONES AND BRYON BUTLER HAVE THOUGHT?

During the days when radios crackled
Through the ether and beyond
The celestial voices of Peter Jones and Bryon Butler
joined us
Through the drizzle, snow and rain of wintry evenings
Football's gracious guardians
Voices of silk, molasses, honey
Radio 2's finest wordsmiths
When Liverpool had Stevie Heighway, Brian Hall
Ian Callaghan on golden thrones
And midweek European Cup nights were minted
And Merseyside was on song
Never walking alone
But what would Peter Jones and Bryon Butler have
composed
To the lyrics of today?
Arteta's Gunners fire their familiar artillery
Against a struggling Newcastle
Perhaps a soulful lament
To the Blaydon Races
Then Gerrard's newly born Villa
On the crest of a wave
Against the team with that palatial home at Selhurst Park
But no chandeliers present now

Crystal Palace stumble over leaden feet
Time to move the silver service into another room
Dust off the decanter
Re-arrange the crockery and cutlery
Palace must be in impeccable condition for Christmas visitors
Butlers in finest suit
And so for Norwich
Hitherto the laughing stock of the Premier League
Neither here nor there
Goalless against a fetching pack of Wolves
Who may not be the Stan Cullis of old
But Hancocks and Mullen
Are now ghosts from Christmases past and days of brilliant gold
So, now the Wolves are howling
Before the nocturnal hour
When once Derek 'the Doog' Dougan, John Richards
And more recently, Steve Ball
Held court to a different tune.

FOR WEST HAM READ THE CLASS OF '65

Far too young to appreciate the seed
Of class and ingenuity
When the claret and blue class of 1965
Held aloft the Cup Winners Cup at Wembley
But 56 years hence
Could the apparition be more real than imagined?
For way back then
Moore, Hurst, Peters
In tandem with Brian Dear, the Stag
Antlers sharp
Johnny Sissons on flank duty
Who reminds you of scissors
That cut inside defenders
A bludgeon and rapier
On this night of nights
Teasing and tormenting
Full of skulduggery and subterfuge
Tomfoolery
And jet heeled propulsion
Alan Sealey, Ronnie Boyce
Whose classical overtures
Pearls of wisdom
Passes
Like sighs of disbelief
Articulate paragraphs on the written page
For Wembley 1965

Perhaps read May 2022
Who knows?
Fairy tale imaginings in the East End foundries
Where the musical docks
Once resounded to the Chicken Run roar
And probably still do in our innermost thoughts
And the Upton Park acoustics
Blasted out melodies that ring again on the glorious night
When the Cup Winners Cup held pride of place
Bobby victorious
Wembley, Wembley.

IN THE MIDDLE OF EUROPE

So, here we are
In the middle of Europa League conferences
Where once the UEFA Cup ruled with the rod of iron
When two legs held us in thrall
But tonight it's Viennese waltzes
For the claret and blue Thames Ironworks
Strauss without stress
And yet it seems to last for an eternity
With group stages as long as vinyl record albums
Drawn out
As now that winter has dawned
And the nights are blissfully comforting
And David Moyes
Enraptured by London Stadium symphonies
That caress the discerning ears of those bubble blowers
Who may think they've seen and heard it all
But then Sunday will arrive
Like a chariot of old City and Pep
Will the Hammers tremble with fear and trepidation?
Or will Sunday be the day
When the mould is broken
And the Premier League champions are toppled from on high
And claret and blue visions reach for the sky?

NEW MANAGERIAL BROOMS — GERRARD, HOWE AND SMITH

New managerial brooms
It only seemed like yesterday
Since they were young saplings
Childish colts spreading the gospel on back streets
Then the fiery furnace of the Premier League
Thrown heartlessly into the fire
Totally immersed in the hullabaloo
And palpitating, nerve shredding first team
Thrown into the pandemonium of fresh-faced debuts
The Premier League, the big time
Then Gerrard, Howe and Smith
Again, stamp their trademark
Stevie G, once a Liverpool monarch
Now in the claret and blue of Villa
Presiding over the oldest of them all
Villa, once of the landed gentry
In football's most imposing drawing rooms and parlours
Then amongst its bejewelled corridors
A footballing powerhouse
Gerrard, in charge of yet more greatness many years ago
But it's been 39 years since the bearded warrior
Peter Withe
Headed the winner against Bayern Munich in the
European Cup Final
Incarnation of another age
But Gerrard

Responsible for the slumbering giant
A player par excellence
Now furthering his education
In more elevated circles
In the more august of red brick universities of the
Premier League
Where degrees of prosperity can often be a poisoned chalice
But Stevie G can sense the ultimate challenge
And never gave more to the cause
A picture of devotion
Then Eddie Howe
From the salubrious breezes of Bournemouth
To the burning passions of Tyneside and Newcastle
Where once Wor Jackie
In his richest plumage
Mined the collieries and seams of Newcastle
Where brown ale was never enough
So, Shackleton, Milburn, Macdonald
All ploughed their furrow at St James Park
Digging for victory
But yielding sore heads and bleak defeats
Sorrowful brows
Mopping fevered anguished foreheads
Nothing since the 1955 League title
Only Joe Harvey
Frantically gesturing at black and white stripes
When Tyneside was the centre of the universe
But defeat in the 1974 Cup Final
To Shankly's mighty composition

The perfect chemical formula
The Liverpool masterclass
And finally Dean Smith
Driven unceremoniously out of his childhood club
The Villa now just a beloved reminder of his past
But back at Norwich
Amongst the rolling fens
Peaty Norfolk smells
The rural cattle
Fertile acres of farmland
Where once John Bond owned a yellow and green revolution
And still Delia demands an extra gallon of sweat, toil
Mouth-watering culinary delights
So, let's hear it for those new managerial brooms
Sweeping the ashes of broken hearts
Fans aching for restoration plays
New Shakesperean acts and dramas
A cabaret of Cups, Premier Leagues and Europe
The big objectives
But only laborious struggles briefly, they hope
When Gerrard, Howe and Smith
Claim the dazzling limelight
Again.

THE SAN MARINO ROUT

England under Gareth, a formidable force
Once again, San Marino crushed like a bulldozer
Monday evenings of cruelty, destruction and carnage
It could have been far more but
Oh, for the suffering of humble little men in red and yellow
Pitiful rag dolls crumpled under the weight
Of England's stampeding feet
Fleet of feet, nimble toes
Delicacy personified
10-0, a festival of mathematics
Wild and wanton goals
By the second, minute
Interminably
Citizen Kane in goal scoring command
Even Tyrone Mings
Amidst the confetti of goal after goal
Festooned all over the history books
Records broken like smashed Greek plates
England poised for another World Cup destiny
The intervention of fate
May well dictate England's form in the deserts of Qatar
But Saka, Abraham, Bellingham
In the first flush of youth
Will offer heart and soul
The full thrust of their gifts
Upon grandiose stages
In the depths of Saudi mid-winter

When Christmas hymnal churches
Pour rhapsodies of religion into the warm embrace of our hearts
Come on, Gareth, with or without waistcoats
A malt whisky or mulled wine
When turkeys and families unite the global themes
So, in England we must trust
That Albania and San Marino
Were like feathers in the wind
Blown away
Like the mercurial speed of Sancho who
Given half the chance
Will demolish the great and good Italy
Because they could be temperamental
Germany because they can only be so thorough and without flaw
Yes, San Marino
Of course
It was a stroll in your park
But Brazil and Argentina
Your heritage and swagger are ready to fall
When Gareth Southgate's men may just, but surely, call.

WEST HAM IN THE TOP THREE

Claret and blue
Within our nervous system
Through the blood vessels
From head to toe
This genetic flight of fancy from the cradle of childhood and now
But West Ham are within touching distance
Of Chelsea and City
Yes, indeed, it is West Ham
Believe it or not
Of that much ridiculed place
When relegation might have been the customary story again
And again
But now it's all very different
In complete contrast
East London
Rubbing shoulders with the dinner party guests
The caviar elite
Amongst the cream of the crop
Today the former Premier League Champions finally vanquished
Undermined
Liverpool stopped in their tracks
This can't be happening to these hitherto trapeze artists
Music hall pastiche
This parody of themselves

West Ham, the soul of our community
Our family of football
Always beaten and defeated
Always that heart flutter of a thousand mediocrities
Never safe or stable
Wobbling like the precarious rock on the cliff edge
Hovering over the precipice
Reliving the days when Bobby, Martin and Geoff won the Cup
But always out in the wastelands and wilderness when trophies called
So, for this devoted fan
Could this finally be our season?
West Ham, divine to behold in November but so far from us
We can hear the summons but not on the day
But perhaps the omens may be just a breath away
It's third at the moment
And the trumpets are silent
If Bowen and Benrahma can execute their faith
In the delicious indulgence of an afternoon in May
Antonio full of bustle and belligerence
Rice whispering subtlety on the ball and into our ears
Oh, West Ham
Let the cavalry charge into our Premier League dreams.

TO FA CUP GLORY

FA Cup first round day
Ah, 'tis the start
Of the meandering, winding journey
To FA Cup glory
Along the rutted paths
The tangle of the orange leaves
Chasing hectically
Darting through the hedgerows
Football at its finest local parklands

FA Cup first round day
The meat and gristle
Of its bone and sinew
Hearty feast and lunchtime fiesta
The FA Cup
It should have its own national anthem
When the supermarket trolley workers
Postmen and milkmen
Down their tools
The long-distance lorry drivers
Dream of Manchester City, United
Spurs, Chelsea and Arsenal
On the glamorous infant days of the third round
When the muck and bullets of the first round of today
Are that first corner swung over with deceptive ease
And we remember Hereford, Yeovil, Sunderland in 1973
Porterfield trapping the ball on that reliable thigh

And leaving Leeds on Cup Final day
With nothing but humiliation for tea

But today is FA Cup first round day
The foundation stone
The first brick
The first layer of cement
Where the FA Cup was born
Where the part timers and the amateurs
Dare with brass neck impudence
To upset the higher proletariat
Where Buxton FC and Sudbury
Trod on hallowed green
There was Canvey Island once
Who could hardly believe that they were TV dignitaries
Rows of terraced houses
Threaded together like Grandma's tea cosies
That settled like the Cup souvenirs that were six pence and a shilling
And fire engines could be seen, cheering from afar
Still the FA Cup once again
The genesis of the season
Crank up the engines
For winter is upon us
Gloves pounding on the terraces
Fans clinging thrillingly to trees
Bobble hats at Northampton Town
The raw chill of the first round of the day
The mystery of the unknown

Meat pie in one hand
Wembley on our minds
We'll always remember this day
For we were there once
When giant killing was the norm
And today is the day it all began
Faded history but very much now.

FA CUP FINAL DAY

The FA Cup, the architecture of our day
Complete and fulfilled
Football's finest column and pillar
A structure of handsome beams
Timber thatched at times
Then the culmination of those dreams
Of cosy pubs where the fug of pipe smoke
Drifted from non-League obscurity
When the third round beckoned
And men of steel, iron
Longed to be free and ready for giant killing themes
When Goliath was a mere boy
Men of tender limb, grace on their mind
Gallantry at their disposal
Ready to topple the impregnable oak that stood upright
Against the boggy marshes and mud
Stained warriors who moved muscle and mountain
To find Wembley in its sights
But then they came in coach and bus in their vocal multitudes
Masses of fans with rosettes, banners of humour
And gentle whimsicality flying across the decades
When time seemed to stand still
Held together with the unity of who they are
Identifiable as the begonia next to me
From Peterborough to Scunthorpe
To Rotherham and Grimsby

Where modest ambitions take up residence at the feet of
the young and old
A feeling of romance
When the fires and flames of hope
Wandered down our lanes
Forgotten by the few who knew victory would be ours
Their scarves ablaze
Passions on the highest platform and summit of
'Abide with Me'
Conducting our triumph on open top buses
Through towns and cities where we used to see
Where families awaited the FA Cup again.

EUROS 2020

So close to Euro victory over England
So, here we are on the verge of something
Indefinable, inexplicable
Mysterious and elusive
The coin we were searching for in dusty attics of yesterday
But oh, not this time, it's only football
Again, it's always been that way
Resignation to our fate
The doomed scenario of gallantry
Runner up
Or nowhere in particular
Humiliated in front of so many folks
Like us, cowering away in the corner
Hiding from the inevitable
But hold on, England are in the quarter-finals
They could or may have to wait their time
To be ordained European champions
Because the scenario is so painfully familiar
If only it had rained for two hours before or one
It would have made such a significant difference
Before the match against you know who
The Germans
Oh, it had to be them
But hey, didn't we see them in our rear-view mirror before?
Or maybe it was a figment of our imagination?
In defeat against the Germans in the dim and distant past
We accepted they were better

But could hardly bear to mention them in the same breath
Because it was just repetitive, insistent
Like the hammering and drilling our neighbours used to make
But then kindly stopped
This time it wasn't mechanical or structured
Or just England throwing in the towel of surrender
Because we'd been to Iceland five years ago
They'd run out of chocolate ice cream
So, we went next door
And hoped it would never happen again
This time, finally, we'd got it right for once
Football lent a helping hand
When viruses were in full spate
That musical band that echoed around Wembley's portals and corridors
We'd given Europe our Citizen Kane
Maguire of this noble manor
When Sterling was worth its weight in gold
Purity of motion and emotion
The currency of today and tomorrow
And eternally
The sprinkling of Rice on this auspicious day
An emperor over all
Then Phillips and Saka broke the mould
Class is permanent
Forever England in the warmest fold.

HONOURS EVEN IN LONDON DERBY

So, it's honours even in London derby
East met North
In gunslingers' shoot out
Swords drawn
Pistols loaded
For bragging rights
Territory claimed as theirs or yours
Flintlock and blunderbuss
Powder kept dry
Perhaps
Sharpened for battle
And then
West Ham met Spurs
Share of the spoils
Predictable draw
Soucek ensures
No Czech mate
Soothes the claret and blue fevered brow
Hitherto West Ham
Sluggish and stodgy
Still lost in the summer haze
Awkward and self-conscious
Perhaps not really paying attention to the teacher
One win, three defeats
And the first draw
Room for improvement

Must sit up straight
For David Moyes
Evening classes
And learn the verbs
Past, present and future
Swot up on your pronouns, metaphors and similes
West Ham, be alive to the new season
Wipe the collective sleep
From bleary claret and blue eyes
Spurs purring
Pompous posturing
Could be accused of masters of the easy pass
So civilised and pleasant to watch
Joyous jewels of passing
Own goal last night
But Conte is one shrewd and knowing coach
Wise in the ways of the world
And then City wear their finest pinstripe suit and bowler hat
Firstly, breaking into the Palace
With four on Saturday
And then six against Forest last night
Who looked lost and without a compass yesterday evening
Send out a search party
To find the Forest clearing
While Chelsea lose their sainthood at St Mary's
Southampton's chapel of joy
Liverpool who hit nine against the Cherries of Bournemouth

Merseyside's morellos
Find yet another Anfield pageant of goals
Painterly passes
A vision in perfect red
Sweetness and light
Then a last-minute winner to save their blushes
Liverpool
Still one of Marlon Brando's contenders near the top
The Premier League
No league like it.

www.ingramcontent.com/pod-product-compliance
Lightning Source LLC
Chambersburg PA
CBHW011956090526
44590CB00023B/3751